St. Anthony's Chapel
IN MOST HOLY NAME
OF JESUS PARISH

1700 HARPSTER ST   TROY HILL
PITTSBURGH PA 15212 4393
412 323 9504

Published By
J. POHL ASSOCIATES
1706 Berkwood Drive
Pittsburgh, PA 15243
(412) 279-5000

ISBN 0-939332-26-4

Designed, composed and printed by Schiff Printing Company; Pittsburgh, PA.

Statue of St. Anthony on Chapel Roof

DEDICATION

This book is dedicated to Saint Anthony, Wonder Worker of Padua, in humble petition that the Chapel erected in his honor may become a refuge and haven for all pilgrim-people who seek to know God, the Father, Son and Spirit, to love Him and to serve Him through the intercession of His Saint!

FOREWORD

We have attempted in this book to help you the reader to come to a better understanding of all that St. Anthony's Chapel stands for. We have tried to do as much research as possible on the Founder of the Chapel, Fr. Suitbert G. Mollinger, and to help you to see all that has made this Chapel such a Special Place for the many years of its existence. We are also trying through this work to open up to more people the history and growth of our Chapel. Many loving hands have kept this Chapel a place of warmth, healing, and spiritual peace for so many. We hope you will enjoy reading this book as much as we did putting it together!

ACKNOWLEDGEMENTS

Many people have helped in this endeavor.
We would like to thank a few in particular.

THE MEMBERS OF THE
ST. ANTHONY'S CHAPEL COMMITTEE

William Fichter, President

Cecilia Guehl, Coresp. Secretary

Carol Brendel, V. President

Dolores Fichter, Secretary

Selma Uhlig, Finances

Sr. Margaret Liam Glenane, SA

Carole Brueckner

Sue Koch

Marge Hoffield

Mildred McGlothlin

Edward Oberst, Esq.

Louis Baysek

Fr. W. David Schorr - Pastor

INFORMATION CONTRIBUTORS

Msgr. Paul Lackner

Greg Weidner

Cecilia Guehl

Dolores Fichter

Kim Baysek

Jennifer Esposito

EDITORIAL STAFF

Fr. W. David Schorr

Louis Baysek

Gregory Jelinek

Chip Kelsch, Photography

St. Anthony's Chapel
MONUMENT OF FAITH

TABLE OF CONTENTS

APPENDICES

EXCERPTS

Some of the dates, times and places in the excerpts are not consonant with the preceding studied data. However, they are incorporated here because they paint a vivid picture of the life and times of Father Mollinger (ZEITGEIST)

(The following articles are taken from the Pittsburg Press,
Pittsburgh was spelled without the "h")

DESCRIPTION OF PHOTOGRAPHS

Cover

Title Page   St. Anthony's Chapel in Most Holy Name of Jesus Parish
1700 Harpster Street; Troy Hill; Pittsburgh, PA 15212-3393

Page iii   Statue of St. Anthony on the Chapel roof

Page v   Interior view of St. Anthony's Chapel

Page 1   Early picture of St. Anthony's Chapel and Father Mollinger

Page 2   The inside of the Chapel, early years

Page 3   The outside of the Chapel, early years

Page 5   Stained glass window of St. Anthony of Padua, in the choir loft

Page 8   Mollinger Family Crest

Page 9   Young Father Mollinger

St. Anthony's Chapel,
Troy Hill, Allegheny, Pa.

Father Mollinger.

INTRODUCTION

Father Suitbert Goedfried Mollinger became the pastor of Most Holy Name of Jesus Parish on July 4, 1868. His twenty-four year pastorate ended with his death on June 15, 1892.

Father Mollinger's special devotion to St. Anthony prompted him to build the Chapel of St. Anthony in the 1880's and to have it enlarged a decade later. The original chapel embraced the sanctuary and the nave as far as the central arch; the wider section of the nave with the niches containing the Stations of the Cross is a later addition. Since there had been some delays and difficulties, the enlarged chapel was not opened formally until the Feast of St. Anthony, June 13, 1892.

As originally planned, the building of the chapel was to have been a joint endeavor, with the people of Most Holy Name Parish providing half the cost and Father Mollinger, the pastor of the parish and the originator of the idea to build the chapel, matching their contribution. Later, when the people of the parish declined to appropriate the large sum needed, Father Mollinger erected the building at his own expense from money he had inherited from his family.

Father Mollinger began to realize his plan for St. Anthony's Chapel in 1880. This picture of the interior was taken in 1892 after the original chapel had been

The Inside of the Chapel, early years

enlarged. Inasmuch as Father Mollinger died without leaving a will, his heirs descended on the chapel and stripped it of its crystal chandeliers, the original black onyx marble altar, candelabras, and all other portable items that could be sold. The chapel and its remaining contents, along with the rectory, were then sold to Most Holy Name of Jesus Parish for thirty thousand dollars. The Diocese of Pittsburgh

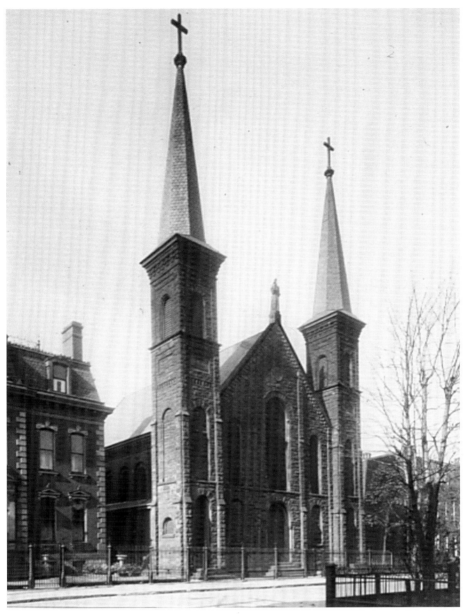

The Outside of the Chapel, early years

lent the parish the money to buy the rectory and chapel, which is the ordinary way church property is obtained. The original sales agreement was signed on June 26, 1893, and personal effects, such as relics and a chalice belonging to Father Mollinger, were signed over by his heirs to Most Holy Name Parish on May 16, 1895.

Because of his devotion to St. Anthony and many other saints, Father Mollinger made numerous trips to collect relics for the shrine he planned in honor of St. Anthony of Padua, and by the time the shrine was finished Father Mollinger had spent much of his personal fortune on the chapel and its relics.

ST. ANTHONY
SAINT OF THE WORLD
THE STORY OF THE CHAPEL PATRON

Fernando (Ferdinand in English) was the Saint's baptismal name. Born in Lisbon, Portugal in 1195, of an aristocratic family, he was probably about 15 years old when he said farewell to the bright worldly prospects that lay before him. Fernando consecrated himself in about 1210 to the service of God as a religious among the Canons Regular of St. Augustine.

But, in the Augustinian monastery near his native city, he was distracted by visits from relatives and friends. After spending two years there, he asked to be transferred to another monastery. He was sent to Holy Cross in Coimbra, a great center of learning and the capital of Portugal at that time.

Fernando devoted the next eight years of his life to study and prayer, immersing himself in Sacred Scripture. This period laid the foundation for his later work of preaching the Gospel.

At Olivais, near his monastery, a few early followers of St. Francis had a little dwelling. Fernando often helped them when they begged for alms. He admired the humble, joyful hearts of these men who cheerfully renounced worldly values. But a far greater sacrifice by these zealous Franciscans proved the turning point in Fernando's idealistic life.

In 1219 St. Francis had sent his first missionaries - Berard, Peter, Accursio, Adiuto and

Stained glass window in the choir loft

5

Otto - to the Muslims. When they urged that the King of Morocco convert to the Christian faith, he put them to death by the sword on January 16, 1220. The relics of these friars were brought back to Portugal and laid to rest in the Church of the Holy Cross in Coimbra where Fernando lived.

Inspired by the friars' martyrdom, he felt called to join the Franciscan community at Olivais in the summer of 1220, taking the name of Anthony, a saintly hermit of the fourth century.

He then set sail for Morocco, but on reaching his destination fell seriously ill and was bedridden for several months. Forced to abandon his plans, he decided to return home. En route, his ship encountered a severe storm and was driven to the coast of Sicily, south of Messina, where Franciscan friars welcomed him and nursed him to health.

In the spring of 1221, a general gathering of some 3,000 Franciscans took place at Assisi, and Anthony went to meet his new brothers. Afterward, seeking God's will, he spent a year in Montepaolo at a mountain hermitage of the friars. Invoking the heritage of his patron saint, he devoted himself to prayer and study in the daily life of a hermit.

God's call to Anthony to enter into the heart of the world came in the summer of 1222. After a priestly ordination of Franciscans and Dominicans at Forli, all gathered for a festive dinner. When no one accepted the superior's invitation to give a talk, he called on Anthony. The friars were soon spellbound by his words – awed by his knowledge of the Scriptures and moved by his eloquence and fervor.

Soon afterward Anthony embarked on his career as a Franciscan preacher that would continue through France and Italy for the next nine years. His sermons often drew large crowds that overflowed town squares and filled vast fields.

The Franciscan final Rule was approved by Pope Honorius III in 1223. Around the same time, Anthony was chosen by Francis to teach theology to his friars, uniting the vision of St. Augustine with the ideals of Francis. This became the special mark of the Franciscan school of theology. Anthony also served as leader of the Franciscans in a region of northern Italy.

St. Francis died in 1226 and was canonized in 1228. From that year onward, Anthony took up residence in Padua but was often on the road, continuing a lasting Franciscan mission of love at work. In his sermons, he defended the Church's teachings against those who rejected them. He spoke out against unjust interest rates and interceded for debtors. He challenged people to give alms to the poor. His stirring works revealed how deeply he understood the problems of the people.

And he strengthened his words with a holy life. "The preacher must, by word and example," he wrote, "be a sun to those to whom he preaches. You are, says the Lord, the light of the world... our light must warm the hearts of people, while our teaching enlightens them."

Perhaps one of the most famous stories about the Saint concerns an appearance of Jesus to him in the form of a child near the end of Anthony's life. He was working on a book of sermons for saints' feasts, while staying at a small Franciscan friary not far from Padua. Anthony's mystical experience of the Child Jesus reflects the central place of the Incarnation of the Son of God in his sermons.

After giving a series of Lenten sermons to the people of Padua in the spring of 1231, Anthony became seriously ill. In the chaplain's quarters of the Poor Clare Convent at Arcella near Padua, on June 13, 1231, he died singing – like St. Francis – his final song, a hymn to Mary.

The children of Padua ran through the streets calling out, "The Saint has died! The holy father has died!" The Church declared Anthony a saint on May 30, 1232, less than a year after his death. Construction of a worthy burial church was soon underway for him in Padua. When Anthony's remains were transferred to the newly completed basilica in 1263, his tongue was found intact. Reverence for the Saint spread from his burial place and has continued ever since.

Undoubtedly, St. Anthony worked many miracles during his lifetime - particularly on behalf of the sick. But he truly became the Wonder Worker of Padua after his death. His fame in obtaining miraculous favors from God has inspired artists throughout the ages. Many images have come to be associated with him as a consequence of this influence - the Child Jesus on his arm, the Bible or a lily in his hand, a loaf of bread extended to the poor.

Anthony's reputation as a 'finder of lost things' assures us that evil cannot overwhelm us, for we have been redeemed by Christ- and that no request is too small for us to make of our heavenly friends, the saints. Contemporary devotion also invokes Anthony as a "finder of lost faith" for those alienated from the Church and as a healer of emotional problems as well as bodily sufferings.

und trozdem

MOLLINGER

THE LIFE AND TIMES
OF FATHER MOLLINGER

MOLLINGER FAMILY

The early life of Suitbert Godfrey Mollinger was set in the Kingdom of the Netherlands. His father, Francois Frederik Mollinger, was born in Kampen on October 7, 1795. His mother, Baroness Dorothea Maria Hellenberg, was born at Tiel, Netherlands, on the 23rd of November, 1795. Suitbert's parents were married at Hampden, a small town north of Maastricht on February 19, 1819.

Young Father Mollinger

The Mollingers had eight children, of which Suitbert was the sixth. The first two children were born in Maastricht where their father was a second lieutenant in the cavalry. The third child was born at Maurik, a stone's throw from Tiel where his mother was born. The fourth and fifth children were born at Mechelin where their father was a soldier.

The sixth child was Suitbert. His birth certificate reads:

"KINGDOM OF BELGIUM
PROVINCE OF BRABANT
COMMON OF CAMPENHOUT"

From the Register of Births of the year 1800 and twenty-eight it appears that on the nineteenth day of April, One thousand eight hundred and twenty-eight is born at Campenhout: "Suitbert Godefridus Mollinger, Son of Francis Frederik Mollinger, First Lieutenant, thirty two years of age, a native of Kampen, Province of Overyssel, living at Malines and of Dorothea Paulina Maria Van Hellenberg his consort, thirty-two years of age, a native of Thiel, Province of Gueldres, living at Campenhout."

9

Suitbert's brother Godfrey was born in 1833 and his youngest sister, Frederique Jeanette, in 1835. All the children were raised in the Catholic faith by their devout mother. Their father, a Protestant, did not interfere in religious matters. In 1838 the senior Mollinger died.

The loss of his father had a profound effect on the ten year old Suitbert. His uncle took the boy on a trip across Europe. Soon after, Suitbert was enrolled in medical school at Naples. He continued his medical education at Rome and Genoa. Suitbert then decided to prepare for the priesthood and began his studies at a seminary in Ghent. His mother was happy for this change of heart, but did not live to see his ordination. She died on September 8, 1854 at Zalt Bommel.

FATHER MOLLINGER'S PRIESTLY YEARS

Suitbert came to the United States to continue his studies for the priesthood; however, it is not known where his ordination took place. Bishop Young of Erie incardinated him into his diocese on April 30, 1859, and assigned him to Brookville in Jefferson County as pastor of Immaculate Conception Parish. The work load was extensive because of the many surrounding mission churches. Father did not see eye-to-eye with Bishop Young on all issues, and consequently decided to join the Pittsburgh Diocese.

The first written information about Father Mollinger in the diocese of Pittsburgh is in the baptismal record of St. Mary's church in McKees Rocks, dated April 30, 1865. Soon after, he was made the first pastor of St. Alphonsus Church in Wexford, which had been founded by the Redemptorists almost a quarter of a century earlier. The parish was composed of Irish and German farmers. In addition to his parochial duties at St. Alphonsus, Father also served a mission church a short distance away in Perrysville. Construction was begun on a church building there, and the cornerstone for the

Wall case containing many reliquaries

10

new "St. Teresa's" was laid by Bishop Domenec. Father worked at St. Alphonsus and Perrysville for over two years before his assignment as pastor of Most Holy Name Parish on Troy Hill.

He assumed his duties on Trinity Sunday 1868. At that time Most Holy Name of Jesus, along with St. Joseph's Church in Manchester, was a mission of St. Mary's, the Benedictine Parish on the North Side. The three churches were named for Jesus, Mary and Joseph, the Holy Family. (Most Holy Name is the only one of the "Holy Family" still a Catholic parish church).

FATHER MOLLINGER'S RELICS AND CHAPEL

There are over 4200 relics in St. Anthony's Chapel. These relics are contained in 800 cases with 525 accompanying documents. Immediately some questions must be addressed about these relics such as: how did they get to Troy Hill between 1868 and 1892? Weren't there only 50 farm families living in the area with a small mission Church in 1868? Over a century ago, wasn't Pittsburgh small and the population sparse? How did this acquisition of relics occur?

When Father Mollinger arrived here in 1868 he brought with him his own collection of relics and more than average facility in procuring relics because he was a well traveled priest and possessed adequate personal money.

THE ACQUISITION OF RELICS: HISTORICAL BACKGROUND

A bird's eye view of what happened in European history sheds more light on the reliquary chapel and how the relics were acquired. During the 19th century European politics was characterized by nationalism and the rise of modern nation states, especially in Italy and Germany where unification took place.

The Italian Risorgimento (resurgence) was an attempt to unify Italy between 1796 and 1870, when the Papal States were annexed. The unification was accomplished through the work of Giuseppi Mazzini, Count Cavour and Giuseppi Garibaldi. Territories that were incorporated into Italy included the Papal States, which the Church had partially acquired centuries earlier in 755 through the Donation of Pepin, the father of Charlemagne. Over a period of 10 years between 1860 and 1870 the pontifical soldiers were defeated and the Church lost the Papal States (the Marches of Ancona, Romagna, Viterbo and Bologna). The monasteries were destroyed and relics were lost, later appearing in pawn shops and other unlikely places. Father Mollinger was able to procure them on his own, as well as through contacts such as Father Hyacinth Epp, a Franciscan provincial who traveled to Europe.

German nationalism manifested itself in an attempt to unify Germany via the Zollverein, an economic union of German principalities. Bismark was the architect of German unification, leading Germany with his "blood and iron" policy and effecting unification through the Danish War, the Austrian War and the Franco-Prussian War.

Bismark began the Kulturkampf or "culture struggle". Distrust of Roman Catholics was a common doctrine among the liberals in the 19th century. The Kulturkampf was an abortive political struggle between the Catholic Church and the Imperial German government. The central issue was state control of educational and ecclesiastical appointments. Bishops and priests were imprisoned and sees were left vacant. The Jesuits were forced to leave Germany. Many felt that precious reliquaries were in jeopardy and thus were sent from Germany for safekeeping, at which time Father Mollinger was able to procure some of them.

MOLLINGER'S DREAM

Father Mollinger had travelled to Europe in 1880, most probably to bring back more relics. Immediately after his return from Europe in 1880, Fr. Mollinger approached the Church committee with a proposal to build a larger church, in which his relics would be housed. Realizing that the parish could not afford the expense of a new building, the committee voted against this proposal. Father Mollinger decided that he would finance a Chapel with his private funds. The cornerstone was laid on the feast of St. Anthony, June 13, 1882, and exactly one year later the chapel was dedicated.

CROWDS COME TO THE CHAPEL

More and more visitors came to Troy Hill and Most Holy Name Parish during the late 1870's because of Fr. Mollinger's work. The size of his collection of relics increased. Father never charged the sick for his medical ministrations; however, many of those whom he helped were very generous in their donations. Father prescribed remedies for them which were filled in a back room of the church. A local pharmacist, Mr. Mangold, continued preparing drugs for

Fr. Mollinger until they became procurable at Mollinger's Drug Co., located near the old Boggs & Buhl's Store on the North Side. If Troy Hill flourished during the 70's because of Fr. Mollinger's reliquaries and the help he provided medically, it became a veritable mecca for the sick after his reliquary chapel was completed. Crowds of people constantly came to Troy Hill for spiritual and medical reasons, and especially for the Corpus Christi processions and the feast of St. Anthony. The *Pittsburgh Catholic* reported that on June 13, 1888 a crowd estimated at 6000 gathered around the chapel in the morning for the 10:30 o'clock Solemn High Mass. From 1888 until 1892 crowds of people continued to inundate Troy Hill. The August 31, 1889 edition of the *Pittsburgh Catholic* states there was an astoundingly large crowd. In 1891 people came weeks ahead of the feast to pray and receive medical attention. In June of 1892, the work of the enlargement of the chapel was completed. It now measured 125 feet long and 50 feet wide. The beautiful wood-carved life-size stations were imported from Germany; new stained-glass windows were put in; the marble for the altar was imported from Rome; a new organ and new bells were installed; and additional fresco work was done by Adolph Steubner.

Father Mollinger

FATHER MOLLINGER'S FINAL YEARS

Father Mollinger suffered continually from rheumatism during the 1880's. As years went on he suffered from dropsy and had to contend with an old rupture which gave him considerable trouble at times. Two prominent physicians, Dr. King and Dr. Peach, attended him constantly. During the last two years of his life he had great difficulty sleeping. Those close to him knew that he did not have long to live.

(The following material comes from the journal kept by the School Sisters of Notre Dame at Most Holy Name Convent. We are not sure which sister wrote this account.)

On June 13, 1890, on the feast of Saint Anthony, there was an extraordinary number of people here. Six thousand, as some newspapers reported, attended on that day. Already several days before, all places of lodging were overcrowded. On the eve of the feast, no more rooms, public or private, were available even for great sums of money. People who came from far away had to spend the night in our school yard and on the church steps. Rev. Suitbert G. Mollinger, for longer periods of time, had half the church filled with the sick, whom he blessed daily, and spoke to each one individually and recommended medicine for them. On the day before the feast, and already some days before, the rooms downstairs, where he usually received the sick, were too small, so that he took them to the classrooms where he tended to them not only during the day but into the night until eleven and twelve o'clock. In consequence of this exertion, Rev. S.G. Mollinger became very ill. He had an attack of the dropsy. The doctors feared for his life. On July 14, he traveled to Atlantic City in hopes of being cured by the ocean air. But he improved only very slowly. When, however, he felt a little better, he pursued even there, in Atlantic City, his favorite occupation, blessing the sick in the same church where he celebrated holy Mass. On August 18, 1890, Rev. S.G. Mollinger returned home, but his health had not improved. He was so weak, that he could not even walk by himself from the carriage into the house. On August 31, we celebrated First Holy Communion for 41 girls and 39 boys, a greater number than ever before in our parish. Rev. S.G. Mollinger did not attend the celebration, he was too ill. In the afternoon, after the services the Communicants went to the rectory where they received their Communion pictures. On Sept. 2, our school started again. On the first day, nearly 60 children entered. The magnificent St. Anthony Chapel had just been completed, but not yet consecrated. On June 11, 1892 our Rev. S.G. Mollinger had been with the Most Rev. Bishop to ask permission for celebrating Holy Mass on the Feast. Since the existing altar of the chapel had been consecrated many years ago permission was granted. Rev. S.G. Mollinger was overjoyed. On June 12, he asked for two Sisters to help him with the decoration of the chapel and the altars. All afternoon, he and the Sisters and several men were busy decorating. He sent for the most beautiful natural flowers and green plants. Rev. S.G. Mollinger did most himself. In the evening, the chapel was most beautiful. Rev. Mollinger couldn't sleep all night. Finally, at 4 o'clock, he arose and at 5 o'clock he celebrated Holy Mass and gave Holy Communion to several of the sick. At 8 o'clock, he was still sitting in our yard when he called me to himself and said to me, how beautiful his chapel was, and that during Holy Mass he had seen St. Anthony who told him to take good care of himself. Several times he called me over and had something to tell me. It seemed

as if he had a premonition that he should see me for the last time. At 9 o'clock ,
he felt already very ill. As every year, very many sick people were here from all over.
Hundreds stood in front of the church and in the street, as the crowd was too large
to fit into the church. As every year, Rev. Mollinger wanted to bless the sick after
the High Mass. But because he felt already very ill, he took along Rev. C. Laengst,
his best and faithful friend. While he was blessing the sick, he felt worse. After he
had finished, he had to be assisted into the house. They had to let him lie on the
floor, so intense were his pains. On June 14, they called Dr. King who diagnosed
his condition as very dangerous, and consulted with three other doctors. On
June 15, the doctors decided on one last means to save his life, an operation. But
it was too late. Rev. S.G. Mollinger died at 2:00 p.m. on June 15, 1892. His
burial took place on June 18 at Most Holy Name Cemetery.

Father Mollinger died peacefully with a crucifix in his hand on June 15, 1892. (See appendix for further information.)

His earthly remains were laid to rest on June 18, 1892, at Most Holy Name of Jesus Cemetery, on Mt. Troy Road; his chapel stands to this day as a monument to his devotion and good works.

THE RECTORY

One of the places dear to Father Mollinger was his home. Many of his days were spent there in prayer and apostolic work. Most Holy Name of Jesus Rectory, the imposing residence which stands to the left of St. Anthony's Chapel, was purchased by Father Mollinger in 1873; after making a number of improvements to the house, Mollinger then sold it to Bishop Domenec for the use of Most Holy Name of Jesus Parish in 1875.

The Rectory is a fine example of the Second Empire architectural style, with its mansard roof and ornate carved sandstone window and doorway pediments.

The interior of the house also conveys an impression of wealth and status. Walls and ceilings feature intricate plaster medallions and colorful stencil work and paintings. The front hallway area houses a grandfather clock produced by Terheyden Jewelers, personal friends of Father Mollinger, an elaborate marble-topped hall piece with a large framed mirror, and an inspiring painting of the deposition of Christ by Von Sil. The master staircase with its Tiffany style window leads to the area where Father

17

Mollinger lived. From the double-shuttered second floor windows on the street-facing side, he could survey his parish, church, school, and other buildings. The rear windows would have afforded a view of his apothecary where his medicines were prepared, as well as his beloved chapel.

The Victorian grandeur of the rectory as it stood in Father Mollinger's day is best retained in the formal dining room. The double wooden doorway of overwhelming dimensions leads from the hallway area into a room of great beauty and elegance, meticulously restored to its 19th century splendor. A gorgeous crystal chandelier illuminates wall and ceiling paintings richly incorporating a variety of fruits and flowers, birds and animals, interwoven in harmonious detail. A glorious mantel of carved and marbleized slate is topped by a ceiling-height framed mirror. Richly carved oak furniture houses a collection of crystal and porcelain decorative and serving pieces. The overpowering ornateness of this room in particular reflects a love for beauty and for the gifts of field, forest, and garden.

THE CHAPEL BUILDING

ARCHITECTURAL STYLE

When Father Mollinger prepared to build his Chapel, he chose a design appropriate to the sacredness of the collection of relics to be preserved there, a space of great beauty to inspire devotion and prayer. A collection of relics as vast as this would be honored in a structure the size and scale of a basilica. As this was not possible, Mollinger chose a building on a smaller scale, along the lines of a chapel royal. Such chapels exhibited the highest quality in materials, design and color.

The original chapel was roughly thirty by thirty feet, laid out in a cruciform plan. Set on a sandstone foundation, it was constructed of thick brick loadbearing walls laid in an English bond pattern and topped with a handsome corbeled cornice. The roof is a hipped design covered with slate and was originally crowned by a cupola glazed with stained glass. This decorative dome was removed at some point in the Chapel's history and replaced by the present skylight. The main entry to this smaller chapel of 1883 stood in the area of the present-day central arch; a smaller entrance was located on the side facing the rectory and can still be seen in the covered passageway.

The later nave addition completed in 1892 defines the architectural style of St. Anthony's Chapel today. Erected to house the large stations of the cross, the extended nave with its bell towers is almost one and a half times longer than the original chapel. The style of the addition is Romanesque, based on Roman design and characterized by rounded arches, vaults and towers, along with thick massive walls of rough cut stone. This architecture communicates the qualities of strength and stability, solemnity, and mystery. Romanesque style was popular in Europe and America from the 1880's until the turn of the century; a fine example of this revived style in our city is the Allegheny County Courthouse and Jail of 1888.

The new facade of St. Anthony's, with its rounded arched openings and blind paneling, flanked by two great square towers, all wrought in rough-cut stone facing, establishes the Romanesque style. Further indications are evidenced in the distinctive voussoirs and the carved interlace patterns in stone above the windows and doors, the carved medallion at the center of the facade and the corbeled bracketed stone work at the tops of the towers and the roof peak. The six stone pilasters that run the height of the facade suggest the masonry buttresses of the Romanesque style and the curved trefoil designs of the heavy doors flanked by two polished granite columns further define this style. Yet the extended proportions and smaller scale of the overall facade convey a lighter, less severe design, a nineteenth-century Victorian adaptation of a twelfth-century Romanesque church.

The nave of the Chapel is built of brick laid three and four courses thick on a sandstone foundation. On the front facade, the brick is clad in a warm-colored sandstone. On the side walls of the addition, the brick is set in an American bond pattern, with a corbeled cornice which follows the design of the 1883 building with an additional decorative course added. The window openings are arched in finished sandstone. The roof and needle spires are of timber construction and covered in slate. The statue of St. Anthony at the roof's front peak is a copper replacement of the original, which was toppled by lightning.

THE RELICS

The relics housed in the Chapel currently number over 4200 and are housed in over 800 relic cases (reliquaries) of various sizes. Furthermore, there are 525 authentic certificates which give the date, name and seal of a Bishop or postulator of the saints' causes, attesting to the authenticity of these relics.

Some of the documents are over two hundred years old. Among the oldest are those dated: August 12, 1716 (bones of St. Frances of Rome No. 236); October 6, 1735 (No. 442); August 12, 1736 (No. 425); April 24, 1744 (St. Philip Neri No. 294); January 17, 1753 (No. 426); April 7, 1762 (No. 357); February 3, 1777 (No. 351); January 3, 1786 (St. Stephen, 1st Martyr No. 300); October 25, 1796 (No. 229). *(Note: A certificate number that is given without a specific saint listed refers to a reliquary that contains many relics.)*

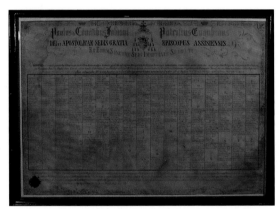

Authenticating certificate for large reliquary pictured on page 28

Among the collection are relics of the apostles, martyrs, confessors, virgins, widows and saintly penitents, as well as particles of the True Cross. The location of the larger, accessible relics can be positively identified, but it is more difficult to pinpoint the location of many of the relics because of the inaccessibility of the reliquaries.

The altars and shrines wherein these reliquaries are arranged are beautifully constructed cases wrought in walnut. Under the tabernacle altar is a precious case, brought from Rome in 1880, containing the entire skeletal remains of the martyr St. Demetrius. *(See photo on page 29.)* To the right and left of the altar are cases containing skulls of martyrs St. Macharius and St. Stephana. In other compartments beneath the statues of the Sacred Heart and the Blessed Mother are skulls of the martyred companions of St. Ursula. Above these same statues are twin cases with a relic for each day of the year, according to the Church

Liturgical Calendar in use at that time. In the center, behind the tabernacle, is a gold case with relics of the saints whose names appear in the First Eucharistic Prayer of the Mass.

Case with recently acquired relics

In the right transept above the side altar is a beautiful copy of the miraculous picture of Our Lady of Perpetual Help, the original of which is preserved in the Church of St. Alphonsus in Rome. At some time after 1928 this picture had been removed from the transept, but was restored to its original site in the transept after the church restoration. On the back of the picture there is a certificate, No. 709, complete with red wax seals and the signature of Nicolaus Mauron, C.SS.R., Superior General and Major Rector, which states: "We affirm and testify that this image of the B.V. Mary faithfully represents and is from the old miraculous archetype, under the title of De Perpetuo Succursu (Our Lady of Perpetual Help), formerly in the church of St. Matthew in the city of Merulana, now venerated in the church of St. Alphonsus Liguori." It is dated 30th October 1880. At the bottom of the certificate there is an added note: "Blessed by Pope Leo XIII."

In the left transept is a beautiful reliquary representing a miniature altarpiece. In this single case there are over seven hundred relics. The large cross in the center contains a particle of the True Cross of Christ, and directly over this cross is another group of relics of the popes who have been canonized.

In the nave are two reclining statues with relics of the saints: St. Mauritius, to the right, and St. George, to the left. Both of these saints are martyrs. There is a shelf above the figure of St. George on which rests a beautiful case built in the form of an altar that has been constructed of relics and contains the names of the saints. Next

Skull of St. Theodore

to it is the skull of the martyr St. Theodore, and directly across the nave of the chapel, above the reclining statue of St. Mauritius, stands a large cross under a baldachino, that contains another particle of the True Cross (see page 25).

Wall cabinets also house hundreds of relic cases, and some of the small reliquaries contain as many as a dozen or more relics. In the middle section of the case on the right wall of the chapel is found a medallion of the Blessed Virgin, an excellent specimen of fine Italian enamel painting.

One noteworthy reliquary, not usually on display in the chapel, resembles a monstrance and has a particle of the True Cross in its center. Around this is a circle with relics of St. John the Baptist, St. Mary Magdalene, St. Lawrence, St. Dionysius, St. Blase, St. Stephen the first martyr, and a shred of the Sacred Winding Sheet. Arranged in the outer rim are relics of St. Anthony of Padua, St. Nicholas, St. Agnes, St. Barbara, St. Sebastian, St. Catherine, St. Cecilia, and St. Lambert. Silver medallions representing these same saints are affixed to the base of the reliquary. Beautiful filigree work and engraving enhance the craftsmanship, and an inscription says that it was made in the city of Aachen in the year 1880 by August Witte. This reliquary has been used since the time of Father Mollinger to bless the people following the novena service in honor of St. Anthony of Padua. *(See back cover.)*

The stained-glass windows in St Anthony's Chapel are the finest of their kind for richness and durability of color. The central window over the choir loft consists of two panels: one depicting the Blessed Virgin Mary as the Mother of God and Queen of Heaven; the other, her spouse, St. Joseph. To the left is a window of St. Anthony of Padua, and to the right, a window depicts St. Catherine of Siena. These windows were made in Munich, Germany, at the Mayer and Co. Works, whose trademark is imprinted on the windows. Above the Stations of the Cross are fourteen more windows that depict eleven Apostles, along with St. Paul, St. Stephen, and St. Lawrence. These were made by the Royal Bavarian Art Institute for Stained-Glass and bear the trademark of F. X. Zettler – Munich 1890.

GREAT BEAUTY

SANCT:STEPHANUS

SANCT:IACOBUS minor.

SANCT:IACOBUS major.

SANCT:PETRUS

SANCT:PAULUS

SANCT:IOHANNES

SANCT:MATTHIAS

SANCT:SIMON

THE ALTAR

Originally, there was a black onyx marble altar situated a few feet in front of the present Communion rail. It had been sold by his heirs after Father Mollinger's death and all trace of it has disappeared.

Black onyx marble is white Italian marble which has been dipped into a solution which penetrates the marble. One is able to see light through the finished product. It was learned that it is no longer being produced after inquiries were made throughout the U.S.A. and Europe to obtain some black onyx marble to make a new altar for the chapel. So the decision was made to

Altar on left side of Sanctuary

Relic case of St. Demitrius under Altar of Repose

settle for black and gold marble for the present Mass altar which rests on bases going down into the ground beneath the chapel.

In the old wooden altar table directly in front of the tabernacle there is a sliver from the table at the Last Supper. A circular glass-topped reliquary has the following inscription: "Ex Sacra Tabula Ultimae Coenae, D.N.J. Christi" – ("From the sacred table of the Last Supper, of Our Lord Jesus Christ"). It is authenticated by certificate No. 502 – 4th article listed – and was given to Father Mollinger by the Minister Provincial, O.F.M., Conv., on June 7, 1890 at Florence, Italy. This reliquary is imbedded in the mensa of the altar, and is regularly covered by the altar cloth.

THE STATIONS OF THE CROSS

The works of art that attract the most attention are the near life-sized carved wooden figures of the Way of the Cross. They are true masterpieces which were imported from the city of Munich in Bavaria and were obtained from the Royal Ecclesiastical Art Establishment of Mayer and Co., Munich.

The Stations of the Cross attract and fascinate the onlooker, so remarkable are they for the anatomical correctness of the figures and realism of their facial expressions. The pain and sorrow visible in the face of Christ is a powerful reminder of the love Jesus showed for us in taking away our sins.

These same Stations remained in their original crates stored in the churchyard for several years until the addition to St. Anthony's that was being constructed to display them was finished. It is sad to note that over the years they have suffered pious abuse such as breaking off the thorns from Christ's Crown and the fingers from statues, as well as neglect and improper care.

THE STATIONS OF THE CROSS

In the early days of Christianity, the faithful retraced our Lord's sorrowful journey; from Pilate's court, through the streets of Jerusalem, to the location of the crucifixion and ending at the burial site on Mount Calvary.

The years following Christ's death brought the universal conversion of great masses of people. Since most people could not make the trip to Jerusalem, the Catholic Church instituted the devotion known as the Stations of the Cross. The fourteen "Stations" help parishioners to recall the principal events of Christ's last hours.

1st   Jesus is condemned to death

2nd   Jesus carries His Cross

3rd   Jesus falls the first time

4th   *Jesus meets His afflicted Mother*

5th   *Simon of Cyrene helps Jesus to carry His Cross*
      (see page 30, middle right)

6th   *Veronica wipes the face of Jesus*
      (see page 31, top)

7th   *Jesus falls the second time*

8th   *The Daughters of Jerusalem weep over Jesus*
      (see page 30, upper left)

9th   *Jesus falls the third time*

10th   *Jesus is stripped of His garments*

11th   *Jesus is nailed to the Cross*
       (see page 30, upper right)

12th Jesus dies on the Cross

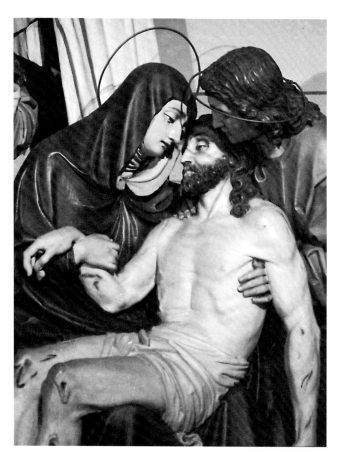

13th   Jesus is taken down from the Cross

14th   Jesus is buried in the tomb

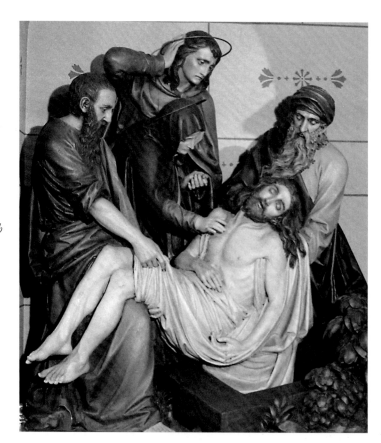

LIGHT FIXTURES

The lighting in St. Anthony's Chapel had never been adequate, so additional lighting was designed and installed during the restoration. Originally, there were crystal chandeliers in St. Anthony's Chapel until their removal and sale by Father Mollinger's heirs. A search was made for pictures that might show the original chandeliers. It had been planned to have copies made of the original chandeliers and mount them in the chapel.

An opportunity presented itself to purchase a chandelier made of Czechoslovakian crystal which consists of three tiers of lights. The source was the Holy Ghost Byzantine Parish in Charleroi, Pennsylvania. On March 12, 1976, the chandelier was purchased and brought to Most Holy Name.

CHAPEL SEATING

The chapel pews are the original ones, some of which are of birch, mahogany and pine. In the course of time a few of the original seats were replaced with pine boards, and in the restoration work they were all stained to a uniform mahogany shade. All the kneelers have been replaced and have cushioned kneeling pads.

THE BELLS

The bells of St. Anthony's Chapel were ordered in April of 1891 by Father Mollinger from the McShane Bell Foundry, Inc., of Baltimore, Maryland. In the belfry next to the parking lot there is a large bell with a deep tone named "St. Anthony." In the belfry by the rectory is a large bell named "St. Francis" and also a smaller bell named "St. Clare." Hence, the bells were named for three major saints of the Franciscan Order.

CONFESSIONALS

The confessionals at the rear of the chapel are works of art. They are artistically hand-carved The kneeling pads and arm rests were refurbished during the course of the interior restoration work.

THE ORGAN

The organ in St. Anthony's Chapel came from Germany. It could well have been a Silberman, but remodeling and other work on the organ over the years have destroyed any positive evidence. The two organ cases are definitely European, and the wood in the organ cases is certainly from Europe.

During the restoration work on the organ, the following information was discovered: The organ was definitely a two-manual mechanical action (tracker action), an instrument of twelve ranks of pipes with a total of seven hundred and sixty-four pipes. The organ was originally hand pumped by a lever on the side of the organ facing the rectory side of the chapel, before electricity was installed in the building. There are men here at Most Holy Name Parish who still recall hand pumping the organ when they were boys.

The organ was obtained second-hand, having seen some thirty-plus years of service before it was installed in St. Anthony's Chapel in 1892. So the organ is actually older than the chapel itself.

SYMBOLISM

The artwork and painting in the Chapel tell the story of our Catholic Faith in symbolic form. This symbolism further enhances the religious significance of the edifice which houses the relics of our ancestors in Christianity. The beautiful hand-carved wooden Stations of the Cross depict Christ's way of salvation to each and every one of us. St. Anthony's Chapel is a repository of religious and cultural art.

Standing in the sanctuary and facing the glass-encased reliquaries, we have on the ceiling, to the right of the reliquaries, the papal emblem with its tiara or triple papal crown. The crozier, or Bishop's staff, is depicted and is symbolic of the Pope as Bishop of Rome. The triple cross represents the fullness of the papal powers. Keys are shown which are symbolic of the keys of the Kingdom of Heaven.

Again facing the glass-encased reliquaries, on the ceiling, to the left of the reliquaries, we have the episcopal emblem. The miter is symbolic of the bishop's authority. The two horns of the miter are an allusion to the two rays of light that came forth from the head of Moses at the time he received the Ten Commandments. The two horns are also symbolic of the Old and New Testaments. The stole is a sign of priestly dignity and power, symbolizing the yoke of Christ and the Christian duty of working loyally for His kingdom, and the hope of immortality. The crozier is symbolic of the bishop's authority and power in his own diocese.

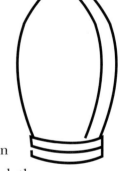

The palm branches indicate that many popes have been martyrs, and the crown represents the fact that many popes have attained sainthood. All that is here signifies victory over sin and death.

Standing between the arch and the sanctuary and facing the right wall we see the richly decorated symbolic representation of the Blessed Virgin Mary, in the phrase "Sancta Maria, intercede pro nobis." It has gold leaf squares containing crosses. Fleurs-de-lys, symbol of the Holy Trinity and the Blessed Virgin, surround the Sancta Maria area. The Fleur-de-lys was derived from the Madonna lily.

A rose, either white or pink, is a common symbol of Our Lady. The usual form is that of a heraldic rose, as seen in the circles running the length of the walls of the chapel. In Christian symbolism, the red rose is a symbol of martyrdom, while the white rose is a symbol of purity. St. Ambrose once wrote that the rose grew in Paradise without thorns. Only after the fall of man did the rose take on its thorns to remind man of the sin he had committed and of his fall from grace, while its fragrance and beauty continued to remind him of the splendor of Paradise. It is probably because of this story that the Virgin Mary is called "a rose without thorns," since she was exempt from original sin.

Again facing the right wall we have at the base of the first pillar the CHI RHO (XP) symbol. This is among the oldest of the monograms of our Lord Jesus Christ. It is formed from the first two letters of the word "Christ" as it is spelled in the Greek language. Christ's name was spelled XPICTOC in ancient Greek capital letters. A horizontal line over the two letters is the sign of an abbreviation.

At the base of the second pillar on the right we have IHS. This symbol can be interpreted as the first three letters of the name Jesus in Greek. Alternately, it has been interpreted as an abbreviation of the Latin phrase, "In Hoc Signo (vinces)," as a reminder of the vision of Constantine in which he saw a cross in the sky together with the words "In this sign you shall conquer."

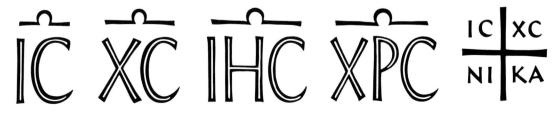

The base of the third pillar has a Patonce cross, a beautiful form of the cross that has been used by decorators and needle-workers down through the ages.

On the ceiling beginning at the arch we have the Eye of God in a triangle. The Eye represents the omniscience of God. The eye within the triangle, surrounded by a circle and radiating rays of light, is used to suggest the infinite holiness of the Triune God. The many scriptural references to the eye of God have led to the use of the eye to symbolize the all-knowing and ever-present God.

"Because the Lord has eyes for the just and ears for their cry; but against evildoers the Lord sets his face"
(1 Pet, 3:1 2).

"The eyes of the Lord safeguard knowledge, but he defeats the projects of the faithless"
(Prv. 22:12).

There is an unusual painting of a pelican above St. Anthony's altar. The pelican, according to legend, has the greatest love of all creatures for its young, because when there is no food it pierces its breast to feed them with its own blood. This legend has come to symbolize Christ's sacrifice on the Cross, because of His love for all humanity, and also symbolizes the Holy Eucharist, in which Christ feeds us with his own body and blood.

Above the center of the arch is a picture of a dove. The use of a dove in Christian art is symbolic of the Holy Spirit.

On the left, facing the arch is a Lamb of God carrying the banner of victory, which comes from Revelation 5,12: "Worthy is the Lamb that was slain to receive power and riches, wisdom and strength, honor and glory and praise!"

On the ceiling of the original section of the chapel we have blue banners emblazoned with the names of the four evangelists: Matthew, Mark, Luke and John. The same theme is carried out on the ceiling of the later addition.

Matthew

Matthew is shown as a Cherub, in human likeness, because he begins his Gospel by tracing the human descent of Our Lord.

Mark

Mark is depicted as a winged lion. It was Mark who opened his Gospel by describing John the Baptizer, as the voice of one crying in the wilderness. Mark also dwells upon the Resurrection of Christ and places emphasis on the royal dignity of Christ.

Luke

Luke appears as the winged ox because of his emphasis upon the sacrificial aspects of Christ's atonement as well as His divine priesthood.

John

John is portrayed as the winged eagle, because John soared to great heights in his contemplation of the divine nature of our Savior.

NEW ADDITIONS

THE CHAPEL SHOP

The Chapel Shop began with the prompting of Fr. Richard Mueller, then pastor of Most Holy Name, in his beginning of the year memo in 1983. In May materials were ordered and the shop opened in June. The Chapel Shop continues to provide a variety of religious articles and books at reasonable prices.

CHAPEL MUSEUM

The first suggestion of a Chapel Museum came in a memo from Father Mueller.

At a meeting on January 19, 1984, a motion was made to establish a museum and that work be started to get the area ready as soon as possible.

The minutes of the October 7, 1984 meeting recorded that the museum was finished and ready to have exhibits put in place.

Parishioners and others were asked to make gifts of items pertaining to the Chapel and Father Mollinger that they had in their possession for display. Items continued to be donated, were catalogued, and put on display. The museum dedication took place on June 10, 1986. The speaker was Father Richard S. Wersing, C.S.Sp., and Mrs. Joan Ivey of the City of Pittsburgh Historic Review Commission cut the ribbon.

Items of religious and cultural interest housed in the museum include a number of crutches, eye-glasses and items left by the faithful who claimed cures of their illnesses.

THE VIDEO

In September, 1992, Paul Ruggieri, a professional cameraman who worked for one of the local television channels, said that he wanted to make a videotape of the Chapel. He volunteered to do this on his own time.

He began work almost immediately and spent countless hours filming in the Chapel over a long period of time. By June, 1994, the project had progressed to a point where he was ready to look for a producer and a narrator. Paul also was able to use the editing room of a friend to produce the finished tape. In October he introduced Chapel Committee members to Chris Winters, a producer for a local television channel, as the producer of the Chapel video.

In April, 1995, Mr. Ruggieri showed part of the tape to Chapel Committee members. At that time he said that he was able to get Ronald Chavis to do the narration.

The video was named THY SAINTS' KEEPER and by November, 1995, it was ready for viewing. The premiere showing took place on November 9, 1995, and to celebrate the occasion local business people, clergy, religious, newspaper editors, museum curators, and all Chapel volunteers were invited.

Since its completion the video has been made available to the Eternal Word Television Network and has been shown a number of times, providing the chapel with widespread exposure from California to Maine.

THE RAMP

The first suggestion that a ramp should be constructed to make the Chapel accessible to the handicapped was made in May, 1991. At a meeting that took place at that time there was a discussion about where a ramp could be placed but no definite action was taken regarding construction.

Eventually it became apparent that a ramp was a necessity and plans were made to proceed with construction. A decision was made as to where the ramp should be placed, measurements were made, and bids for construction were solicited. The bids that were received from various contractors were submitted to the Diocese of Pittsburgh for consideration, and permission was given to spend the necessary funds for construction of the ramp. The contract was awarded to Schrauder Construction Company and work began on June 19, 1996.

The ramp was completed in September, 1996, and the dedication ceremony took place on November 1, 1996, the feast of All Saints, a fitting date considering that relics of many saints repose in the Chapel. Fr. W. David Schorr, the current Pastor, asked Fr. James Wehner, a parishioner, newly ordained, and a past tour guide for the chapel, to do the blessing.

IN RECENT YEARS...

Over the years, St. Anthony's chapel, while much beloved by friends and parishioners, had fallen into a state of serious disrepair. At the request of the pastor of Most Holy Name of Jesus Parish, Father George A. Benton, Bishop Leonard granted permission in 1972 to raise funds for the restoration of the chapel. A stipulation was attached specifying that no parish money would be used, and parishioners themselves should contribute only in addition to their usual support of parish programs and properties.

Father Benton gave local historian and parishioner Mary Wohleber permission to form a committee for the chapel fundraising, and she was joined by parishioners Thomas Koch, Pauline Stauber, William Fichter, Cecilia Guehl, Arthur Roos and James Spagnolo in this effort. Bingos, winetasting parties, concerts, and raffles were held, and donations were requested through a vigorous mail campaign and by word of mouth. Committee members collected the old roof slates, silkscreened a commemorative message on each, and sold these as mementos. Even the school children helped with funds raised through backyard fairs and sales.

When adequate funds had been raised for the first phase of restoration, the chapel was closed as work began on the exterior. Fundraising continued, and work commenced on the chapel interior. By the time both phases of restoration were complete, almost a quarter of a million dollars had been raised to cover all necessary expenses.

The completely restored chapel was reopened on Sunday, November 27, 1977, with a mass at which Bishop Vincent M. Leonard presided. Since fundraising needs had been met, the committee which served this purpose was disbanded.

In August of 1982, the Chapel Committee was reactivated by the new pastor, Father Richard Mueller. Mary Wohleber agreed to chair the committee members who responded to the pastor's invitation, and the business of collecting funds to maintain the shrine was again taken up. A time of growth and involvement had begun.

On June 13, 1983, the centennial of the reliquary chapel was celebrated with a festive eucharist, again presided over by Bishop Leonard. The chapel gift shop was also opened the same month in the property across the street from the chapel. Space was prepared for organizational purposes in the same building, and the chapel office was ready for use by February of 1985.

Planning began around this same time for a small museum connected with the chapel, and the Father Mollinger Museum became a reality. Dedicated on June 10, 1986, this collection of religious artifacts and memorabilia is housed on the second floor of the Chapel Shop. Highlights include a collection of crutches once left at St. Anthony's, several personal possessions of Father Mollinger, and bottles which once contained the medicines prepared according to his formulas.

By 1988, eleven years after the initial restoration, the Chapel had begun to show signs of deterioration, and steps were undertaken to reverse the situation. During the winter of 1988 and spring of 1989, roof repairs were made, waterproofing and interior painting and cleaning were accomplished, and fire and security systems were updated.

In July of 1989, Father W. David Schorr was appointed pastor of Most Holy Name of Jesus Parish. At his suggestion, Sister Margaret Liam Glenane, S.A., began her ministry at St. Anthony's in August of 1991. Just before this, in May of that year, Bishop Donald Wuerl appointed Father Dennis Delle Donne as Administrator pro-tem of the Chapel, who was so installed a month later.

A special week of celebration marked the one hundredth anniversary of the opening of the expanded Chapel in 1892. Auxiliary Bishop William Winter presided at the opening mass on June 8, and on June 13, 1992, the actual anniversary date, Bishop Anthony Bosco of the Greensburg Diocese, formerly a Northsider, presided at a triumphant and crowded eucharist. The chapel shined through a wealth of floral decorations, and centennial banners hung inside and out. The hundredth anniversary of Father Mollinger's death was observed at a mass celebrated by Auxiliary Bishop John McDowell on June 15, two days later. After mass, Father Schorr and a group of committee members placed a wreath of flowers on Father Mollinger's grave, and offered prayers there.

In the mid 1990's, Sister Margaret and volunteer Betty Chernosky undertook the gigantic task of cataloging the relics. After they finished the actual search and cleaning of each relic case, a volunteer, Lynn Wietharn, put all the information in the chapel computer. From this data, Fr. Schorr sorted the records and checked spelling of saints' names and created a file to get as much information as possible.

Thanks to their efforts, a list of the relics and a description of their location is now available in published form, "SAINTS & BLESSEDS" WHOSE RELICS ARE IN ST. ANTHONY'S CHAPEL - a tremendous contribution to the history and work of the Chapel.

St. Anthony's Chapel continues to thrive, by the grace of Almighty God and the efforts of dedicated pastors and of many volunteers who serve as attendants and tour guides, operate the gift shop, and serve lunch to tour groups. It is our hope that devotion to St. Anthony and stewardship of the relic chapel built in his honor will continue, and that future generations will care about the shrine which has been sanctified by the prayers of the faithful for over a century.

APPENDIX A.

CHRONOLOGY

1795	10-7-1795 Francois Mollinger born at Kampen, Holland
1795	11-23-1795 Dorothea Hallenberg born at Tiel, Holland-Gelderland
1815	Kingdom of Netherlands established by Congress of Vienna
1828	4-19-1828 Suitbert Mollinger born at Kampenhout, South Brabant, Kingdom of Netherlands
1838	12-30-1838 Francois Mollinger died at Ech En Weil, Gelterland
1844	Suitbert's medical education at Naples, Rome and Genoa
1852	Suitbert entered seminary at Ghent
1854	9-8-1854 mother died at Zalt Bommell
1859	4-30-1859 Incardinated into Erie Diocese
1859	Assigned to Brookville, Jefferson County - Pastor
1864-5	Entered Pittsburgh Diocese at St. Mary's, McKees Rocks
1864-5	Pastor at St. Alphonsus in Wexford
1866	Constructed a church at mission in Perrysville, St. Teresa.
1868	June 1868, left Wexford
1868	Trinity Sunday - Pastor at Most Holy Name of Jesus Parish for 24 years until his death 6-15-92
1868	8-26-1868 Began construction of Church
1868-74	Completed and furnished church - began construction of new school -
1875	School staffed by Notre Dame Sisters - built new rectory
1868-92	He used his medical knowledge to help his parishioners and others who sought his aid. Added to his collection of relics from Italian and German sources.
1882	6-13-1882 Cornerstone laid for Chapel
1883	6-13-1883 Chapel dedicated - first section
1892	6-13-1892 Second half dedication
1892	6-15-1892 Fr. Mollinger dies
1893	Rev. John B. Duffner became our next pastor.
1893	Beginning with April (1893) services were held in the chapel because the walls for the addition to the church were broken through. "On July 7, the renovated church was blessed. It was so beautiful that one could hardly believe that this was the same church." (from the SSND JOURNAL)

TRANSITION PERIOD

1974	Restoration
1984	Museum was begun on top floor of bookstore.
1982	Centennial celebration was held for first section of Chapel
1992	Centennial celebration was held for completed Chapel
1995	New relics were procured from Rome by Rev. James Wehner.
1996	Video of Father Mollinger and the Chapel made by the Chapel Committee.
1996	Ramp added to the chapel to give access to all visitors

APPENDIX B.
KINGDOM OF THE NETHERLANDS
1815-1839 – NORTHERN PORTION
The Council of Vienna formed THE KINGDOM OF THE NETHERLANDS in 1815.

Its dissolution was completed in 1839

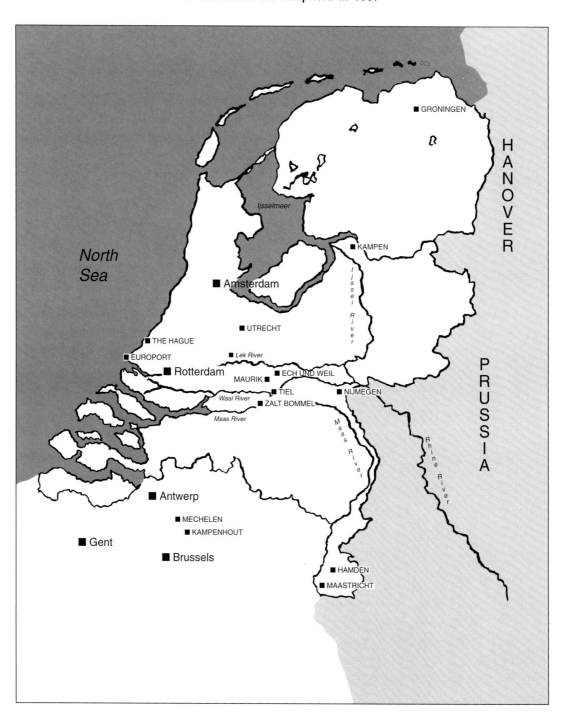

APPENDIX C.

THE MOLLINGER FAMILY TREE

Francois Mollinger born at Kampen 10-7-95

Dorothea Hallenberg born at Tiel 11-23-95

Parents married at Hamden 1818

Francois Mollinger Jr. born at Maastricht 6-10-19

Francoise Mollinger born at Maastricht 11-10-20

Ernest Mollinger born at Maurik 4-24-21

Maria Amelia born at Mechelen 10-17-23

Johann Theodore Mollinger born Mechelen 3-31-25

Suitbert Mollinger born at Kampenhout 4-19-28

Godfroi Mollinger born at Zalt Bommel 9-9-33

Frederique Jeanette Mollinger born at Amsterdam 10-24-35

Father died at Eck Und Weil 12-30-38

Suitbert in seminary at Gent 1852

Mother dies at Zalt Bommel 9-9-54?

APPENDIX D.

EXCERPT FROM
BRIEF BIOGRAPHICAL SKETCHES
by Father Andrew A. Lambing, pp. 316-317

Not long after his appointment to the pastorate of the church Father Mollinger placed a statue of St. Anthony of Padua in it, and devoted his energies to the propagation of devotion to this household saint. The people took to it with a good will, and under his enthusiastic leadership, it soon began to attract attention, and draw devout clients from far beyond the limits of the parish. He also began to collect the relics of saints, and in a short time had one of the largest collections in the country, which continued to increase till the time of his death, when it is said to have been one of the largest in the world. In time it grew to such proportions that it could no longer be accommodated in the church and his residence and he built a spacious and elegant chapel for its reception on lots he purchased in his own name, which was dedicated to St. Anthony of Padua, his favorite patron, to which they were removed, and where they still remain. The extent of the collection almost surpasses belief; and it was natural that some persons should express a doubt with regard to the genuineness of some of them. Considering the centuries that have passed since many of the saints died, the number of places and hands through which relics so often pass, and other points relating to many of the relics of saints, it would be extremely difficult to affirm that every single one in so large a collection is genuine; but this is far different from making sweeping assertions. After years of acquaintance with Father Mollinger, I feel confident that no one who knew him would believe that he would allow himself to be imposed upon, or that he would fail to make use of such precautions as piety and prudence would suggest to authenticate the relics that came into his possession from time to time. Besides, he possessed special advantages for making such a collection, and the times were favorable. It is astonishing what a person can accomplish in any particular line if he devotes unremitting attention to it. We frequently find evidence of this in the most unlikely places. Father Mollinger's hobby, if you like the expression, was the collection of relics, and he was enthusiastic in working it. He was possessed of means; he was acquainted in Rome, and some of the principal cities of Europe; he had persons who were always on the alert for relics that might be secured; monasteries in Germany and parts of Italy were being stolen by the government, and their inmates with all the government did not see fit to confiscate, were being sent adrift; and the best opportunity that could be desired was presented for securing relics, second-hand books, etc. I myself bought a folio Bible printed by Anthony Koberger in 1478, at Nurenburg, for forty-five dollars. In the light of these facts, it is not at all to be wondered at that Father Mollinger could have succeeded in collecting so large a number of relics. Many another person with his means, his enthusiasm and his opportunities could have perhaps effected as much.

APPENDIX E.

EXCERPTS FROM
OLD ALLEGHENY REVIEW

SKETCH OF THE LIFE AND WORK OF FATHER MOLLINGER
The Celebrated Priest/Physician of Troy Hill
with a description of his
Famous Original Prescriptions

INTRODUCTION

In presenting this book to the public we do so with the fullest confidence that it will prove of inestimable value to all who suffer from the various diseases described if they but follow its directions.

This country is being continually flooded with various forms of advertising matter proclaiming the virtues of innumerable remedies of more or less value.

In nearly every case you are called upon to believe these advertisements without any further proofs of their truthfulness than numerous testimonials from people you never saw or heard of.

This is not the case with the remedies recommended in this book. In the entire history of medicines no remedies have ever been offered to the public that were entitled to the entire confidence of the people so thoroughly as these are.

Never has a manufacturer of a proprietary medicine even been able to substantiate his claims by such an array of indisputable facts.

The thousands upon thousands of wonderful cures, performed by these remedies, have already moved the whole civilized world to its very depths, and the name of Father Mollinger has gone down in history as that of one of the world's greatest healers of disease.

The newspapers of the world vied with each other in honoring Father Mollinger and proclaiming his works, and Allegheny City became the Mecca of reporters, hither came thousands of afflicted people of all nationalities and creeds. All were treated without cost. Father Mollinger was broad in his philanthropy: Protestant, Catholic, Atheist and Pagan were treated alike.

This priest-physician issued in seven years over 80,000 prescriptions, the most of these in the last two years of life, as his fame spread. What healer of disease ever equaled this?

Two of the most essential points in compounding this vast number of prescriptions lay in the skill of the druggist and the purity of the ingredients used. To perform this responsible work, Father Mollinger selected Druggist A.F. Sawhill, of Allegheny, Pa., and it was by him that every one of these prescriptions were filled. The originals are on file with him at present.

So particular was Father Mollinger in this respect that he wrote his prescriptions in a cipher to which only Mr. Sawhill had the key.

Owing to the great fame of Father Mollinger, others, since his death, have placed upon the market various so-called Father Mollinger remedies. The fallacy of the claims made by the manufacturers of these nostrums is evidenced by the fact that they advertise a single remedy to cure a list of ailments for which Father Mollinger issued no less than thirteen distinct prescriptions.

In other words, they prey upon his reputation, they claim to accomplish more than he could. The public is cautioned against the wares of such sharks.

The original prescriptions are all on file with and all genuine Father Mollinger remedies bear the name of, A.F. Sawhill, Druggist, No. 187 Federal Street, Allegheny, Pa.

> *OIL CITY, PA, June 13. -"Father Mollinger, to whom so many surprising cures are ascribed, was in Oil City twenty-nine years ago, and it is credited by reputable citizens that he then effected the cure of Daniel Sweeney, who was believed to be on the point of death with black diphtheria."*
>
> *– Pittsburg Leader, June 14, 1891*

It is said that there are 2,400 disorders to which the human frame is subject.

FATHER MOLLINGER

In ancient times the supernatural and the miraculous controlled the world. Everything was explained, but nothing was understood. In those days a dead saint was better than a live physician.

St. Valentine cured Epilepsy; St. Gervasius was exceedingly good for Rheumatism; St. Michael for Cancer; St. Jude for Coughs and Colds; St. Ovidius restored the Hearing; St. Sebastian was good for the Bites of Snakes and the Stings of Insects; St. Apollonia for Toothache; St. Clara for any trouble with the Eyes, and St. Hubert for Hydrophobia.

It was known that the doctors reduced the revenues of the church; that was enough. Science was the enemy of religion.

Father Mollinger was a conspicuous example of the change that has been wrought in the attitude of the church towards medical science. In him were united the priest and the physician. His great fame was due to his success in alleviating the physical sufferings of humanity. Whatever of his marvelous healing power may be attributed in some minds, to his office as a priest. Father Mollinger himself attributed the wonderful cures to the use of the remedies he prescribed.

The Rev. Suibertas Goddfried Mollinger was born on a quiet frontier estate between Belgium and Holland, about 64 years ago. His father was of Dutch extraction, a gentleman of landed estate, and a Protestant. His mother was of the house of Hallenburg, a family of royal blood. She was a devout Catholic and raised her children in that faith.

In Father Mollinger's early years an uncle took him through the continent and finally left him in Italy to study medicine. After studying two years in Naples, he studied in Rome and afterwards in Genoa.

In his studies of medicine he displayed an excellence in learning beyond any student of his various classes. He had a phenomenal memory, which, united with years of study, under the ablest professors in the greatest medical universities of the world, explains his wonderful knowledge of medicine.

After completing his studies, he returned home. Very soon afterwards at the earnest solicitation of his mother, it is said, he entered the seminary of Ghent and studied for the priesthood for four years. During his term at Ghent, he formed the acquaintance of an American bishop in search of missionary volunteers.

Of his many classmates who offered their services for this work, he was the only one who kept his promise when it came to the final point. He landed in New York towards the end of 1854, and went direct to Cleveland, Ohio, where he entered college under the direction of Bishop Rabe (Rappe).

In February, 1857, he was ordained a priest and assigned to the then diocese of Pittsburgh, now diocese of Erie. Under Bishop O'Connor and Bishop Domenec he did missionary work through the State of Pennsylvania for eight years.

During this period of his life he endured many hardships and was often compelled to ride forty miles in answer to a call from some dying person.

In 1865 he was appointed to the rectorship of Wexford and Perrysville. In the latter place he built a church and served his congregation for three years.

It was on Trinity Sunday, twenty-four years ago, that Father Mollinger came to Mt. Troy as pastor of the parish of the Most Holy Name of Jesus. He was the first priest that ever preached on the hill in Allegheny City, where St. Anthony's shrine now stands.

Under the supervision of Father Stiebel, the pastor of St. Mary's and also vicar-general of the diocese, Father Mollinger started building his church. By order of Bishop Domenec he took charge of the place.

Just prior to his appointment as pastor of Mt. Troy, his uncle in Belgium died and left him 20,000 francs a year out of his estate. After considerable litigation for a number of years, he obtained his income and some other money which had been tied up in the courts.

With this he commenced to build his famous St. Anthony's shrine, since then he has expended $237,000 on the chapel and its contents. Not long after starting to build his shrine several relatives died leaving him large properties. He never kept any accounts, and it is impossible to estimate with any degree of exactness how much he was really worth.

Father Mollinger died at 1:50 PM, Wednesday, June 15, 1892, from the effects of a rupture sustained many years ago. This was aggravated by overwork. He literally worked himself into his grave in his efforts to relieve the sufferings of his fellow beings.

At 10:30 o'clock, on the morning of June 17, Father Mollinger's body was removed from his residence to the chapel on Mt. Troy, where, for so many years, he had been accustomed to receive the people and cure them of their ailments and infirmities. Here the body lay in state until the following day, the church being kept open all night to accommodate the thousands who wished to view the remains.

With the most impressive services, all that was mortal of the famous priest-physician was laid in its last resting place in the cemetery of the church of the Holy Name. It was the greatest funeral procession ever seen in Western Pennsylvania.

The news of Father Mollinger's death fell like a thunderbolt on the thousands that were waiting for treatment at his hands. They had waited day after day in expectation that each succeeding day would find the great healer able to resume his work. Some would not leave until they saw his remains laid in the grave.

In all his work, Father Mollinger acted as a priest and physician to his congregation, but his fame began to spread about ten years ago, until his name and fame were as wide as the universe. A careful estimate, made by those closest to him, places the number of patients who visited him at 323,750.

The story of his healing has been told in every land, and his home on Mt. Troy stood out to the unnumbered sick like the star of Bethlehem to the bewildered shepherds. As many as fifteen thousand people have visited Mt. Troy in a single day.

The world has never witnessed such gatherings of afflicted humanity as have assembled at this Mecca of the sick. Many came thousands of miles; they came from all countries; some were so poor that, when they reached Pittsburg, they had not money enough left to buy food, and this good man often caused refreshments to be issued to the crowds in waiting to see him.

The street cars of the lines leading to Mt. Troy were often called ambulances by their conductors, so crowded were they at times with the maimed and the sick. Early dawn would find the vicinity of the church crowded with distorted humanity.

The neighborhood was filled with boarding houses and restaurants. Large amounts of money were offered the attendants of the priest-physician, as bribes, to gain admittance out of turn. The thousands of wonderful cures performed by Father Mollinger are now a matter of history.

> *"It is variously estimated that from, 12,000 to 20,000 people visited Mt. Troy, June 13, 1891, either as spectators or in the hope of receiving treatment from Father Mollinger."*
>
> *-Pittsburg Leader , June 12, 1891*

Selected Description of Cures

Chorea or St. Vitus Dance. This disease is characterized by incomplete control of the muscles of voluntary motion by the will, giving rise to irregular, tremulous and often ludicrous actions. It has been quaintly designated "Insanity of the Muscles."

The disease occurs most frequently in young people, between the ages of six and fifteen. By degrees all the voluntary muscles become afflicted and the child finds it impossible to keep quiet. It usually affects one side of the body more than the other. The movement is always more severe when the patient is being watched.

Sold by druggists. Price, $1.00 per bottle.

Dyspepsia. This is a disorder that is becoming alarmingly prevalent and undermines the entire health. When Dyspepsia takes her seat upon the throne of the stomach, she invites countless other disorders to the banquet, robs life of all its charms, and is a prolific breeder of a species of animal called "cranks."

Life in a lunatic asylum would be paradise to life in a community inhabited solely by confirmed dyspeptics. The causes of this disorder are almost as numerous as its victims.

Fight dyspepsia as you would a snake in the grass. It will shorten and embitter your life. Use Father Mollinger's Original Prescription and you will suddenly find yourself minus a very choice variety of evil spirits.

Sold by druggists. Price, $1.00 per bottle.

APPENDIX F.

EXCERPTS FROM
IMMACULATE CONCEPTION PARISH BOOK
Material prepared for book for Immaculate Conception Parish, Brookville 1996

REV. SUITBERT G. MOLLINGER, 1858-1864

Born at Mechlin, Belgium, son of the prime minister of the King of Holland; educated at Amsterdam, Naples, Ghent; studied medicine for a time; Seminary training at St. Vincent's College at Latrobe; hearing impaired a result of diphtheria as a child; assistant to Father Ledwith with headquarters in Brookville in 1858; made pastor—resided at the Farley House on the corner of Barnett and Madison Streets (the site of the present gun shop) in 1859; attended to Corsica, Crates, Sligo, south-eastern Clarion County, and all of Jefferson County – mostly farming districts and at the little blast furnaces that dotted the counties; was nearly six feet tall, strongly built, stern face, with long heavy beard, determined disposition; produced a patent medicine (Mollinger Medicine Company, N.S. Pittsburgh, Pennsylvania) which the country people hailed as a miracle cure; disagreed with, Bishop Young over the academy in Corsica, left the area and diocese and entered the Diocese of Pittsburgh in 1864; named pastor of Most Holy Name Church at Troy Hill in 1868. His chapel, full of relics, has become a place of pilgrimages.

An interesting story is told about Father Mollinger when he was attending to some out-missions under his charge. One Sunday morning, he set out with his satchel containing the vestments and everything required for Mass, and walked twelve miles on a hot summer day to Carr's Furnace (near New Bethlehem) for a second Mass. On entering the house, he was so exhausted that he fell unconscious on the floor. After a time, he regained consciousness, celebrated Mass, attended other duties awaiting him. In those days, priests and people fasted from midnight before receiving Communion.

APPENDIX G.

EXCERPT FROM
THE BALTIMORE CATHOLIC MIRROR

SATURDAY, JUNE 18, 1892

Reverend S. G. Mollinger, Pastor of the Church of the Most Holy Name, on Troy Hill, Allegheny City, just across the river From Pittsburg, died at 2:00 o'clock on Wednesday, afternoon June 15th. On Monday during the St. Anthony's day exercises he became ill and had to be carried to his house. A difficult surgical operation for rupture of the stomach was performed. He was born in Holland of well-to-do Parents and sent to St. Vincent's College, Westmoreland County, Pennsylvania to be educated for the Priesthood. He was ordained at St. Vincent's. He also studied medicine at this College. In 1869, he came to Mount Troy and has been there ever since, and has become widely known for performing many miraculous cures both by medicine and a relic of St. Anthony. He was seventy years old. He charged nothing but patients were at liberty to contribute to the poor box of his church. St. Anthony's Day was the time for the popular pilgrimage. This Celebration occurs on June 13th. The crowd this year on that day was especially large. Last Monday 10,000 pilgrims bowed before the shrine. There were afflicted people from every part of the country. Australia even had its representatives. Not a tenth part of the visitors could get inside the church, but camped outside on the pavement and under the trees waiting to be healed. The new chapel is the greatest repository of saintly relics outside of the ancient churches and monasteries of Italy. Many of them were given to Father Mollinger by the Pope in honor of his works.

EXCERPT FROM
THE BALTIMORE MIRROR

SATURDAY, JUNE 25, 1892

Remains of Father Mollinger were buried on Saturday morning, June 18, in the cemetery of the Most Holy Name, Mount Troy, Pennsylvania. Six thousand persons attended his funeral and a long procession followed the body to the grave. Services were conducted by Rev. Wall, assisted by a score of priests.

APPENDIX H.

EXCERPT FROM
PITTSBURG PRESS
NORTH SIDE, ST. ANTHONY'S CHAPEL – JUNE 5, 1892

The annual pilgrimage to the shrine of St. Anthony has again commenced, and the many boarding places clustering about the little chapel are rapidly being filled with visitors. The [fame] of Father Mollinger the venerable priest-physician, has spread to all parts of the continent, and he now numbers among his patients invalids from nearly every state and territory in the union, as well as from Canada and British Columbia.

Some of these visitors have traveled hundreds of miles to get here. So firm has [been] their assurance that Father Mollinger can help them that many of them have spent every cent of money they had for railway fare and have suffered the greatest discomforts by traveling day and night in crowded day coaches in their efforts to put themselves under the priest's influence and receive the blessing as soon as possible.

An interesting scene is now presented in the neighborhood of Father Mollinger's little chapel. The residence of the priest, the chapel, and many of the boarding places are located on Hazel Street. In the rear a hill slopes gently downward into a beautiful valley, and from the porches of the residences an interesting panorama of the surrounding hills and valleys is afforded. In decided contrast is the view from the river front. Instead of a clear atmosphere and the bright hills covered with foliage, can be seen nothing but a huge cloud of black smoke that seems to settle continually over the city, with here and there a church spire, a smoke stack or tower projecting through the cloud.

The streets are lined with wide-spreading shade trees, and invalids in roller chairs wheeling themselves about, others limping along on crutches can be seen at all hours of the day, regaling themselves with the pure air and bracing breezes that sweep over the hill. Occasionally one meets a blind person feeling his way along the curb with his trusty cane, but the greater majority of the invalids spend their time sitting about the porches of the boarding places reading, writing or engaged in conversation. Were the tell-tale crutches, canes and roller chairs absent, one might take the place for a quiet summer resort.

It is in the morning after breakfast that this colony of invalids awake into activity. As early as 5 o'clock they begin to move toward the chapel to mass or for prayers and then take seats in the reception room to await the appearance of Father Mollinger, in hopes of being the first to be ushered into his presence. It is in the waiting room that the invalids have to display the utmost patience and fortitude. Here some of them sit in one position for hours waiting for a chance to get a seat nearer the priest's consulting office. It is estimated that during the past two weeks there have been fully 600 people in the church and waiting room every morning.

Few remarkable cures have been reported thus far this season and it may be due to this fact that the influx of visitors is not nearly so large as last year. They are coming every day, however, and this week will add hundreds to the list every day.

Last year the total attendance on St. Anthony's day was nearly 20,000. Of course this number included many visitors from different portions of the city. This year it is thought the number will be above 12,000. The cottage keepers are preparing for a larger number, however, and some of them have erected sheds and opened their residences to use as dining rooms when the guests begin to swell in numbers.

Several invalids who claim to have been benefited by Father Mollinger during the past few weeks were seen by the Press representative yesterday. The case of Miss Annie Moore of Oil City created considerable comment. Last winter she was stricken with the grip and was very ill for several weeks. During her illness her eye sight failed, and when she recovered she was unable to distinguish a single object. She consulted several physicians at home and in this city, but they could give her no encouragement. She finally decided to go to Mount Troy and see Father Mollinger. She has been there but a few days and says she can now see as well as ever. Miss Moore has a brother who is an engineer on the Baltimore & Ohio road, and she has been stopping at his home in Glenwood.

Miss Julia [Quill] came from far off Portland, Ore., to see the priest-physician. Her complaint is spine disease, for which she has been suffering for the past five years. She says she has already been benefited. She cannot remain until St. Anthony's day and will finish her treatment at home.

Michael O'Regon, of Youngstown, O., has been suffering from an injury to the spine contracted while lifting a heavy load. He says: "I came here a week ago. I was unable to walk and could scarcely move my body; now I can run and jump and kick as high as the next man," and suiting the action to the word, he vaulted over the porch railing to the street below, a distance of nearly eight feet.

During his stay on the hill the reporter was given an opportunity of seeing the interior of the new stone chapel, which has just been completed. A fair representation of the exterior of the building is shown in an accompanying illustration. [Quality too poor to scan.] He was shown through shaded lawn to the side door of the chapel.

As a place of worship the little chapel is well worth seeing. There is something very European in its internal as well as its external appearance. With its single aisle and model choir, it seems truly reminiscent of the old English cathedral. A splendid statue of St. Anthony, of Padua, stands in the center of the building near the vestibule containing the relics. It stands on a pedestal of Italian, brilliant and Kentucky marbles, intermixed with cut onyx in variety. On either side are the altars of Joseph and the virgin in delicate rosewood, finely polished. These are about 12 feet high, and the statues, which are miniatures, are encased in glass. Around the aisle are the stations of the cross; magnificent works of art. The story of Calvary is told with life-size pictures of the Savior's sufferings, and reflect with brilliancy from the gorgeous nichings in which they are placed. Each station is a life representation of the way of the cross, carved from Linden wood. The figures were imported from Munich at a total cost of $28,000. There are 7,000 relics in the building. They are placed in cases which line the walls of the chancel. There are many relics of St. Anthony, such as fingernails, pieces of wood from the shoes he wore, and there are mites of the dresses worn by St. Mary and St. Theresa. The ceiling of the building is beautifully frescoed. The nave is lighted from windows on the second tier, while the whole is devoid of galleries, except that set aside for the use of the choir. On this gallery stands a new organ, which has just been built.

The church was first opened to the public yesterday morning, when Father Mollinger administered the blessing upon his patients. The formal dedication will take place next Saturday with elaborate and impressive ceremonies. On the Monday following will be St. Anthony's day.

APPENDIX I.

EXCERPT FROM
PITTSBURG PRESS
NORTH SIDE, ST. ANTHONY'S CHAPEL – JUNE 12, 1892

SHRINE OF ST. ANTHONY

Thousands of Anxious Visitors Expected To-Morrow. Father Mollinger's Resort.
Many People Who Have Come from a Distance to Be Cured of Disease. Interesting
Services to Be Held in the Little Chapel.

The pilgrimage to St. Anthony's Shrine on Mount Troy has ceased and at sunset to-morrow night the vast assemblage of invalids will begin to disperse. For weeks past they have been coming in from all sections of the country, until all the boarding places in the vicinity of Father Mollinger's chapel have been taxed to the utmost capacity to receive and accommodate them. In fact there are so many visitors they have sought shelter in private families or are being cared for by relatives or friends.

To-day an air of anxious expectancy pervades the place. Bright face, cheerful and hopeful, the invalids are waiting the dawn of to-morrow when they will be permitted to bow before the shrine of St. Anthony and reverently press their lips to the relics placed before the altar. They will attend mass as usual this morning and will go to the confessional at 2 o'clock this afternoon. The rest of the day they will spend in prayer and supplication, so that on the morrow they may be healed of their infirmities.

An animated scene will be presented in the little chapel to-morrow. From early morning until evening there will be hours of excitement. Besides the hundreds of invalids now at the boarding places clustered about the chapel, thousands of visitors will go up from the two cities and it is expected that fully 12,000 people will take part in the ceremonies of the day. For the first time the organ in the chapel will be opened, and will lead the chorus of celebrants in appropriate chants which have been selected for the occasion. Father Mollinger will conduct the ceremonies assisted by two priests from the city. In the afternoon he will bestow the blessings on the heads of the multitude.

It was expected that the new chapel would be dedicated today, but is was stated yesterday that the time of the dedication has been postponed indefinitely.

A representative of the Press paid a visit to Troy Hill last evening. He found Father Mollinger seated on he steps of his residence perusing an evening paper. He looked up sharply as the reporter stepped toward him and thinking the reporter was one of his patients, he exclaimed, "I cannot see you now. I am too tired to do anything more today. Tell my secretary your ailment."

"I wish to inquire about the dedication of the new chapel," said the reporter.

"Oh, well, it will not be dedicated to-morrow; I cannot say just when the event will take place. This new chapel is an addition to the old one. The old chapel was dedicated years ago and the new portion will not be dedicated until it is finished. It is not quite ready. When all is in readiness the bishop will take charge and will dedicate the new part of the chapel with the usual ceremonies. Nothing but the regular mass will be held to-morrow. "

The venerable priest-physician was kept busy all day yesterday receiving visits from his patients. His office is now located in the rear of the little frame building which was erected last week opposite the new chapel on Hazel street. The main room of the building, 45 x 25 feet in size, is used as a chapel and waiting room for patients. On the right, in front, is the entrance to Father Mollinger's consulting room and the left is the exit door. All day long this little chapel was filled, and one after another the patients passed in and out of the office. Some came out with beaming faces, while others seemed downcast and forlorn. At 5 o'clock in the evening the chapel doors were closed, and disappointment was depicted on the faces of many who failed to see the physician.

Among the visitors to Mount Troy from a distance are Henry Quinlan and wife of Deer Lodge county, Mont.

"I came to take care of my husband," said Mrs. Quinlan. "About five years ago he was stricken down with pneumonia. Since then he has been scarcely able to do anything. We are engaged in stock raising and have a large ranch in Montana about 40 miles north of Butte City. We also have a ranch down in Wyoming. Altogether we have about 2,500 cattle and horses on the ranch at home. We make all our shipments to Chicago. It is a good, healthy country out there, but I thought a change might benefit Mr. Quinlan, and then I have hopes that Rev. Father Mollinger may do something for him. We will travel for two or three months in the east before returning. We were induced to come here by our friends after hearing of the remarkable cure of Mary Ryan, a young lady residing at Helena, Mont. She came here about three months ago and was almost crazy with epileptic fits with which she was afflicted. She stayed here about a week and went home completely cured."

Walking back and forth in front of one of the boarding places was a handsome looking young man. He carried a long cane reed in his hand and always swung it out before him in walking. He has been blind for the past 10 years. To the reporter he gave his name as Frank D. DeMarsh and said he resided with his parents at Little Rock, Ark. His father accompanied him.

"Father Mollinger says my eyes are all right only the nerve is paralyzed," said Mr. DeMarsh. "He thinks I will get well. I was stricken blind about 10 years ago and had just gone through the junior class in the high school. I have always congratulated myself that I got so much of my education before losing my sight. Since then I learned to manufacture brooms and can earn my own living in a broom factory. I have faith that God will be merciful to me in my affliction, and that I may be cured."

Another touching sight was that of a crippled boy being carried about the streets in the arms of a man. The boy was James Hearn of Brazil, Ind. About 11 months ago he was stricken with rheumatism and has since been unable to walk. When he came to Troy Hill he could not move either hands or feet. Now he can move his body and arms freely and says he will walk before he goes home. His father is a commercial traveler and is here with him.

One of the most cheerful patients in the little colony of invalids is John Richards, of Canton, 0hio. He is blind, and is also suffering from a nervous affliction.

"Well, John, what success to-day! " asked a friend as John walked down from the consulting room. "Oh, he gave me great encouragement."

"That's good."

"Yes, he said that I would get well. Glad of it too, for I would like to get cured."

APPENDIX J.

EXCERPT FROM
PITTSBURG PRESS
NORTH SIDE, ST. ANTHONY'S CHAPEL – JUNE 13, 1892

MECCA OF INVALIDS

Throngs Crowding Around the Shrine of St. Anthony Hoping for Restoration.
Many Unable to Obtain Admission to the Chapel.
Some Stirring Incidents.
A Force of Police on Duty to Preserve Order.
Many of the Sick Disappointed.

Father Mollinger's little kingdom was a scene of animation today that was most interesting to not only the people of his faith, but as well to those of people of other denominations. Mount Troy had a holiday today. The patron saint, St. Anthony, was to be honored. Dead, yet living in the heart of the great church, the commemoration of the anniversary of his birth brought thousands to the little chapel which the venerable father has given a world-wide renown. A stranger, suddenly thrown upon the scene witnessed this morning, would wonder what it was all about. Carriages came driving up to the chapel from all directions; from them were carried into the chapel the sick, the lame, the blind; around in the vast crowd that had gathered, walked many who used crutches, many whose faces bore upon them the expression that only can come from suffering. All day yesterday the people came- the boarding houses, which are as plentiful almost as the number of visitors, were crowded. One young man, a wealthy resident of Washington city— Bohrer Von Orendorf—was there to be cured of paralysis. He was before the shrine of St. Anthony last year and had received, as he told the writer this morning, great benefit; he was not yet cured but he expected to be; one woman was there who had come all the way from Australia. She was certain that she would return cured of her ailment. It was noticeable, however, that the crowds that thronged to St. Anthony's chapel to-day were not as large as they were in former years. Most of the people were from Pittsburg and Allegheny; the visitors from abroad were not numerous.

The services today commenced with the early mass at 6 o'clock. The chapel was crowded and the service an impressive one. At 7:30 the mass for the repose of the soul of the patron St. Anthony was held. At both services the chapel was crowded, with hundreds unable to get in. It was not until 10 o'clock, however, when the high mass was to be celebrated, that the throng grew large. For an hour before mass commenced, the street half-way to the next square was packed. In the chapel yard was a crowd that suffocated almost. One woman fainted and had to be carried out to a shady place where she received medical attention. Cripples were thrown about, crowded, and many who were not cripples were in danger of becoming so, so eager were the multitude to enter the sacred edifice. Officers of the church and five policemen were needed to preserve order and to see that those entitled by reason of their infirmities to enter the church and receive the blessing, were allowed to do so. In the crowd were Detectives Steel and McKelvey, of Allegheny, who were watching for pickpockets. Before 10 o'clock they had ordered two men to take a walk and not show themselves while the services were being held on Mount Troy. It was after 11 o'clock when Father Mollinger, having sprinkled holy water over the heads of the congregation, came out among the crowds to do the same. To-day he gave only the general blessing; to-morrow he will give the individual blessings, and each day thereafter for three weeks.

Back of the chapel, in a little yard, was observed a sight that once seen cannot soon be forgotten. All have read of the pool of Siloam. How eagerly the sick and diseased awaited the troubling of the waters; but here to-day in that little yard sat mothers with sick infants, young girls, walking on crutches, boys, crippled and paralyzed, old men suffering with rheumatism—dozens of these people awaited the coming of Father Mollinger. They sat upon the hard, hot ground; leaned against the high wall that enclosed the yard, and all had their eyes turned toward the door where at any moment might come their healer. It was a dreary wait, but there was on each face an expression of patience. There was no disorder; there was, of course, considerable crowding about the entrance to the old chapel, but it was a disorder that naturally arose, not from any desire on the part of the people to make the occasion an uncomfortable one.

While everything was impressive inside of the church, outside it was a curious scene. Lemonade and fruit booths were as plenty as at a circus; yells of "Here's your lemonade, 1 cent a glass," were heard on all sides. Nearly every house had a sign upon it, "Meals at all hours, by the day or week." Upon numerous porches sat invalids who knew that today they could not get to see Father Mollinger and receive his benediction. They were trying to make themselves comfortable, evidently waiting for the morrow, when their chance would come to kneel before the father. At 2 o'clock this afternoon, an impressive scene was witnessed. The crowd had greatly increased and the mass in the church was one that always draws a crowd. The usual general blessing was bestowed on the people. The street cars did a large business today. Every arriving car was crowded to its utmost capacity. The saloons on the hill were also well patronized. It took a great many barkeepers to supply the thirsty customers.

Father Mollinger will hold daily services for three weeks, blessing all who come. It was noticeable to-day that most of the visitors were children or women. Very few men were seen. For the next three weeks Mount Troy will be a busy place.

Transcribed by dc.

APPENDIX K.

EXCERPT FROM
PITTSBURG PRESS
NORTH SIDE, ST. ANTHONY'S CHAPEL – JUNE 15, 1892

STILL VERY ILL

Father Mollinger Can See No Patients This Week.
Many Had to Return Home.
Those from a Distance Remaining for a Blessing.
A Funeral from the Church.
The Solemn Services Attended by the Afflicted.
All the Visitors Are Disappointed.

This morning Father Mollinger gave instructions to his clerk to announce to the hundreds of waiting patients at the little church on Mt. Troy that there would be no audience granted to them before next week. Father Mollinger is ill. Even in the most urgent cases it is stated by his clerk that it is not advisable for him to see them.

Of course, there was disappointment when this announcement was made. Many of the people had come from a far distance; with the exception of a very few they were poor. They had hard work to raise the money to bring them here, and now that they are compelled to spend another week before they can get relief or a blessing, it is very hard on them. Some of them, not having money enough to do this, went home to-day, their visit to the shrine of St. Anthony, a failure in so far as a cure was effected.

The boarding house keepers, however, are still doing a good business. Every shady porch this morning seemed to be full of patients. Aged men walked about under the shady trees of the church yard, led by boys—they were blind. One young man who was blind was led by a cripple who had to use one crutch, but he was eyes for the stalwart man who could not see.

The writer met a lady leading a little girl. The little one was suffering from a nervous disease, and her mother had to watch her closely. "She has been this way," said the mother, "since she was eight months old. I know Father Mollinger can cure her. I only wish we could get to see him," and the mother's eyes filled with tears.

There are several hundred patients on the hill awaiting the blessing, which they hope will put them again in good health. But nothing will now be done until next week.

At 9 o'clock this morning there was a funeral from the church. Adam Hock, a man of 58 years of age, had died, and the services were held at the church. The

70

deceased had been a prominent member of the little church and the funeral service was a very impressive and solemn one. The mass for the dead was celebrated by Father Meyer assisted by [Fathers] Danziger and Griffin. The church was crowded and many beautiful floral emblems were seen. The singing of the choir, composed for the most part of children, was excellent, and Organist Holmes rendered some beautiful solos. Had it not been for this service, which many of the sick and crippled attended, there would have been very little to write about to-day, and a very small crowd would have been seen about the little chapel.

Father Mollinger passed a good night, but it is said he is too weak to even walk about the room. His condition, however, is much improved since yesterday. On Monday morning he arose very early, and the different services and the large crowds of people coming to the chapel had a prostrating effect upon him.

He will, as he has said, be ready for active work next Monday.

APPENDIX L.

EXCERPT FROM
PITTSBURG PRESS
NORTH SIDE, ST. ANTHONY'S CHAPEL – JUNE 16, 1892

THE DEAD PRIEST

FATHER SUITBERT MOLLINGER
BORN: 19 April 1828
DIED: 15 June 1892
BURIED: Most Holy Name Cemetery

A Sorrowing Throng of People Assembled on Mount Troy.
More Patients Arrive.
They Hear of the Demise With Profound Grief Arranging for the Funeral.
Priests That Will Participate in the Services.
The Body Now Lying in State.

A deathly silence reigned on Troy Hill this morning. Few people were on the streets and the general aspect about the neighborhood of the residence of the late Father Mollinger was one of sadness. Every now and then people could be seen inquiring for the home of the priest-doctor, and the looks of disappointment which overspread their countenances when told that Father Mollinger was dead were distressing to behold. Some of them had not even known of his illness and their feelings of disappointment were mingled with those of sadness at the departure of a spirit so full of kindness for the suffering multitudes.

Last night and this morning people arrived from Philadelphia, Toronto, Montreal, and many other points, and came to see Father Mollinger this morning. A gentleman and his little son from Coulterville were among the visitors this morning. He had brought his little boy here to be treated by Father Mollinger for an ear disease. A growth of flesh had almost covered the boy's left ear, and the hearing was almost destroyed. Eminent physicians had told him that nothing but a painful surgical operation would cure the boy. This the lad would refuse to listen to, and the parents not wishing to force him to undergo the operation had decided to ask Father Mollinger to heal him. The gentleman had expressed his bitter disappointment and went to the residence, hoping at least to get a last look at the remains of the dead priest.

At 2 o'clock this afternoon the remains were taken to the Church of the Most Holy Name where they will lie in state until 9 o'clock Saturday morning, when the funeral services will be held. The C. M. B. A. will guard the remains tonight, and the Knights of St. George will perform that duty tomorrow night. At the funeral services Father Wall will be the celebrant of the requiem mass. Rev. Peter Kauffman of St. Peter's will assist. Father Langst, of the Congregation of the Holy Ghost, will officiate as sub-deacon. Father Schwab, of Sharpsburg, pastor of St. Mary's and of the Congregation of the Holy Ghost, will preach the sermon in German. Father Wall or someone else appointed by the bishops will preach the sermon in English. Father Williams of St. Anthony's church, Millvale, will be master of ceremonies. Father Dangelzer will have charge of the chants.

The will of Father Mollinger has not yet been found. It is believed to be in his safe, or directions there where the will may be found. Father Wall was the only one who knew the combination of the safe, and an employee of the Barnes Safe & Lock company tried in vain to open it. Another attempt to open the safe will be made at 4 o'clock this afternoon, and if the combination cannot be found it will be broken open. There will, according to an authentic source, be some surprises when the will is read. People who thought they would benefit by the will on account of standing in close relationship with the dead priest will be sadly disappointed when the disposition of the estate is learned. It is thought he has made few individual bequests and the major part of his fortune will go to the church and various charitable institutions. Father Danziger said this morning that Father Mollinger kept all secrets relating to the disposition of the estate by his will safely locked within his own bosom and when any one would venture to inquire how he would distribute his property, Father Mollinger would always give the inquirer to understand that such matters concerned no one but himself, and that was about all the satisfaction that could be had on that subject. Father Danziger said Father Mollinger had told him none of his estate should go to anyone outside of the church or the United States. This statement is remarkable in view of the fact that all of Father Mollinger's relatives reside in the old country. It is thought by others that the property owned by him in Europe will go to his relatives there.

No one but Bishop Phelan knows who will succeed Father Mollinger, and it is doubtful if the bishop has determined who shall take his place. Father Danziger said there were only one or two priest physicians in this country, and that whoever succeeds Father Mollinger will continue the blessings for the sick, but no cures will be effected other than through the faith cure. No medicines will be administered hereafter. Many people who, learning of Father Mollinger's serious illness, remained in the city hoping that by next week he would be able to attend to their needs, left the city this morning. It was a rather curious crowd of invalids and cripples that met at Union Station this morning to take trains for different directions for their homeward journey. Never again, perhaps, will there be such crowds come on the annual pilgrimage to the shrine of St. Anthony to be healed of their infirmities.

APPENDIX M.

EXCERPT FROM
PITTSBURG PRESS
NORTH SIDE, ST. ANTHONY'S CHAPEL – JUNE 17, 1892

LYING IN STATE

The Body of Father Mollinger Placed in the Chapel.
Several Thousands View It.
The Services To-Day Were Imposing but Brief
Arranging for the Funeral.
Priests Who Will Take Part in the Exercise.
No Will Has Yet Been Found.

At 10:30 o'clock this morning the remains of the late Father Mollinger were taken from his residence into the little chapel on Mt. Troy, where for so many years he had been accustomed to bless the people and cure them of their ailments and infirmities.

Most impressive was the procession that preceded the remains. Around the residence, on the streets and on the porches of houses was one of the largest crowds seen on the hill since Monday. Most of the people were women. The men were working today. Sitting on the benches in the church yard were rows of women and children, patiently awaiting the procession, and the church was filled with those who were anxious to see the dead priest placed before the altar. Policemen were on hand to keep the crowd back from the entrance to the residence in which he had lived. One stood at each gate and all were obliged to stay out. None but those who had business were permitted to enter the residence. A post-office carrier came with a large batch of letters and papers for Father Mollinger. They were left at the house as usual. Just before the procession from the house, two mother superiors came out. Several priests were there too, but only the pallbearers and Dr. King were allowed, of all the people, an entrance. The remains of Father Mollinger have not been well preserved owing to the extreme heat, and it would have been difficult to keep them over tomorrow. The casket in which they lie is a very plain, but rich one. It is trimmed with black, has solid silver handles, and on the lid is a small silver image of Christ on the cross.

At 10:30 the chimes in the new chapel of St. Anthony began to ring and the bell in the old chapel was tolled. It was a signal that the body would soon be removed to the altar, where it is to lie in state till to-morrow. The crowds began to gather. The street in front of the late residence of the priest was packed. From the parochial school came a procession of boys and girls which numbered 300. They were preceded by Father Meyer and the altar boys who bore the crucifix and candles. All marched around the house and came out on the street, forming two divided lines, through which the coffin was to be borne by the pallbearers.

The strong voice of Father Meyer was heard reading the service for the dead. A few moments later the voices of the singers rendering the De Profundis, psalm 129, gave notice that the procession had begun. The crowds of people uncovered their heads. The form of Father Meyer, in his official robes, was seen coming from the door, preceded by the vested altar boys bearing incense and the crucifix. Several singers accompanied Father Meyer, assisting in the chant.

The body in its casket came next. The pallbearers were Michael Creuner, C. Pappert, H. Krancer, Andrew Weiblinger, Jr., Emil Andrews and Adolf Hepp. All the last named were trustees of the church.

Arriving at the church the choir sang an exultabant and a miserere. There was a prayer and the service for the day was concluded.

There was but little decoration in the interior. A few vases of cut flowers were placed by the chancel, and several potted plants. The casket containing the remains was placed in front of the chancel.

The church will be kept open all night and the body will be guarded by young men from the various societies in which the late priest was interested. Thousands will view the remains.

Tomorrow there will be a great funeral. Rev. Father Meyer has charge of the funeral arrangements. It is expected that Bishop Phelan, Rev. Father Ward, Rev. Father McTighe, Father McDermott, Father Griffin, Father Murphy and Father Danziger will be the celebrants of the last rites of the church. The services will begin at 9 o'clock to-morrow morning. Solemn high mass will be celebrated by Father Wall, with Father Kauffman of St. Peter's as deacon, and Father Langst as [sub-deacon]. Father Schwab, of St. Mary's, Sharpsburg, will preach the funeral sermon, and Father Danziger will chant the service. The remains will be interred in the Holy Name cemetery. It is expected that the services will last at least two hours. Thousands will be present.

"No will has been found as yet," said the late private secretary, Adolph Hepp, this morning.

"I have been told by an intimate friend of the late father," said a gentleman this morning, "that there is a will and that Father Mollinger had told his friend that he had one. He also is reported to have said that the new chapel was his own and that he proposed to do what he pleased with it. I believe someone knows where the will is and that after the funeral it will be brought forth. I am of the opinion that there will be a surprise in store for someone when it is read."

One of the most important questions that engage the mind of the clergy and the people is, who will succeed the dead priest. It was said to-day by several who are in a position to know that Father Dangelcer will succeed Father Mollinger. It is stated that for several years he has studied medicine, and that he is well versed in the study.

Many of the afflicted people who came to Mount Troy from a distance will remain till Monday. One young man who came with his mother from Junction City said that his mother had received a blessing just before Father Mollinger took sick, and that for the first time in years she was able to walk without crutches. Others who came too late will remain to do honor to the dead.

APPENDIX N.

EXCERPT FROM
PITTSBURG PRESS
NORTH SIDE, ST. ANTHONY'S CHAPEL – JUNE 18, 1892

LAID IN THE GRAVE

Impressive Services over the Remains of Father Mollinger.
Immense Crowds Present.
The Chapel Filled and Thousands Fail to Get In.
The Funeral Procession.
One of the Largest Ever Seen in This Vicinity.
No Will Has Yet Been Discovered.

Solemn and impressive were the services held this morning at the Church of the Most Holy Name, on Mt. Troy. They were the last rites over the remains of Father Mollinger, an earnest priest, an esteemed citizen and a good man.

The funeral exercises of Father Mollinger were largely attended. Early this morning people began to assemble on Troy hill, and long before the hour appointed, 9 o'clock, the auditorium was filled with people. Those outside formed in procession and were allowed to pass up the aisles and view the remains before the exercises began.

People continued coming, and soon there was a vastly larger crowd outside than inside the church. It is estimated that fully 6,000 people were in and about the church during the services.

It was touching to see the reverence paid by this mass of people to the departed priest. They knelt on the ground, in the churchyard, on the sidewalk and on the streets. Not a word could they hear of what was said, but from long attendance upon church services knew well the services that were being conducted in commemoration of the departed. Little groups of persons stood about street corners with sober countenances, and in low tones praising the merits of Father Mollinger. There was no business done on the mount this morning save by the street car companies and a number of extra cars were put on to accommodate the increased traffic. Everything seemed unusually quiet on the hill. In spite of the big crowds the six policemen and two detectives of the Allegheny force who were on duty had little to do. The greatest difficulty the officers had to contend with was in keeping the people from thronging into the church, which was already crowded beyond the point of comfort.

Among the more noted priests who came to attend and take part in the services were: Father Carroll, a Capuchin priest, of Butler; Father Peter Kauffman, of St. Joseph's church, Manchester; Father Ward, of Mercy hospital; Father McCabe, of Bloomfield; Father J. Jordan, Rochester; Father F. A. Bush, Altoona; Father P. Clement, St. Mary's church, Allegheny; Father P. Benough, St. Mary's church, Allegheny; Father Laurence Werner, CSSR., St. Philomena; Father C. Rebham, St. Philomena; Father Dennis, C. P., St. Paul's monastery, South Side; Father [O'Conner], Mt. Washington; Father J. S. Schramm, St. George, South Side; Father John Bausch, Homestead; Father Krogmamm, Wexford; Father Julius Kuenzer, Perrysville; Father P. J. Quilter, Mansfield; Father Suhe, East Liberty; Father Duffner, South Side besides Father Meyer, Father Wail, Father Wilhms, Father Danziger, Father Lengst and other priests who took part in the ceremonies.

When the hour of 9 arrived the chanting the De Profundis took place and occupied the time until 10 o'clock, when requiem high mass was celebrated, Father Wall celebrant. Father Kaufmann, of St. Peter's church officiated as deacon, and Father Lengst as sub-deacon. Father Danziger had charge of the chants. Father Schwab, of St. Mary's church, Sharpsburg, a life-long friend of Father Mollinger, preached a short funeral sermon in German, and he was followed by [Father Bush], of Altoona, who spoke in English. Both addresses were impressive and earnestly delivered. The [absolution] was pronounced by Father Bush. The services at the church were concluded at 11 o'clock. The solemn concourse of people then formed in procession, and the march to the grave was begun. Three young men bearing the American flag draped in mourning headed the procession. They were followed by 300 school children, who only went part of the distance to the cemetery and then turned back. Then came the literary society of the Most Holy Name, the O.M.B.A., Knights of St. George, and the St. Anthony Literary society. Another American flag and the papal flag were home in the procession, and then came the altar boys. They were followed by carriages containing the priests, sisters of mercy, and friends of the deceased.

The cemetery of the Most Holy Name where the interment took place is three miles from the church of that name. Notwithstanding the distance a large crowd followed the procession to the grave. At the cemetery Father Wall conducted the ceremony of absolution. The Dies Irae was sung by the choir and after the benediction the sorrowing multitude returned to their various homes.

The absence of Bishop Phelan caused considerable comment. He was expected to be present and take part in the exercises. As the hour approached for the funeral the other priests began to fear he would not be present. A carriage was sent for him and under the circumstances it was thought he would certainly come. The carriage returned without him. He sent word by the driver that he was out the day before and was tired and could not.

Attorneys Hartje and Mueller, formerly counsel for Father Mollinger, have searched diligently for the missing will, but no trace of the document has yet been discovered. Every scrap of paper having any indications of being the missing document is carefully examined, and if there is a will it will shortly be found. It is thought there is surely one in existence and the only question is where to locate it.

APPENDIX O.

DIRECTIONS TO ST. ANTHONY'S CHAPEL

FROM THE NORTH

Follow I-79 south to I-279 south. Take the 28N/East Street exit. This will bring you to a STOP sign. Proceed straight to the third traffic light (Rt. 28). Turn left onto Rt. 28 and proceed to the second traffic light. At this second traffic light, you will turn left onto Chestnut Street. Almost immediately, you will come to a traffic light at Troy Hill Road. *__Turn right onto Troy Hill Road from Chestnut Street. Follow this road to the top and pass North Catholic High School on the left. Follow street around corner to STOP sign (right turn can keep moving). Proceed right onto Lowrie Street. Follow Lowrie Street to third street on left (Claim Street). Turn left onto Claim Street and follow as far as the street goes. Claim Street turns right into Harpster Street. The Chapel is about 1/2 block up on Harpster Street on the left.__

FROM THE WEST (AIRPORT)

Follow Parkway to the Fort Pitt Tunnel. As you exit the tunnel, stay in the left lane. Follow signs to I-279 north. Three Rivers Stadium will be on your left. Bear right after the Stadium to follow sign to I-279 north. Take Chestnut Street exit off of this roadway. At exit, turn left at STOP sign onto Chestnut Street. Proceed straight to second traffic light (Troy Hill Road). *Follow directions in* **bold type*** *above to Chapel.*

FROM THE EAST

Follow Parkway into downtown Pittsburgh. Take the Northside/Three Rivers Stadium exit. You will then follow the signs to I-279 north. Three Rivers Stadium will be on your left. Bear right after the Stadium to follow sign to I-279 north. Take Chestnut Street exit off of this roadway. At exit, turn left at STOP sign onto Chestnut Street. Proceed straight to second traffic light (Troy Hill Road). *Follow directions in* **bold type*** *above to Chapel.*

FROM THE SOUTH AND DOWNTOWN PITTSBURGH

Take Rt. 51 south through the Liberty Tunnels. Cross the Liberty Bridge and take Seventh Avenue to Grant Street. Turn right onto Grant Street. Follow Grant Street to Liberty Avenue to the 16th Street Bridge. Turn left onto the 16th Street Bridge. Cross bridge and proceed straight ahead to the third traffic light (Troy Hill Road). *Follow directions in* **bold type*** *above to Chapel.*

MAP TO ST. ANTHONY'S CHAPEL

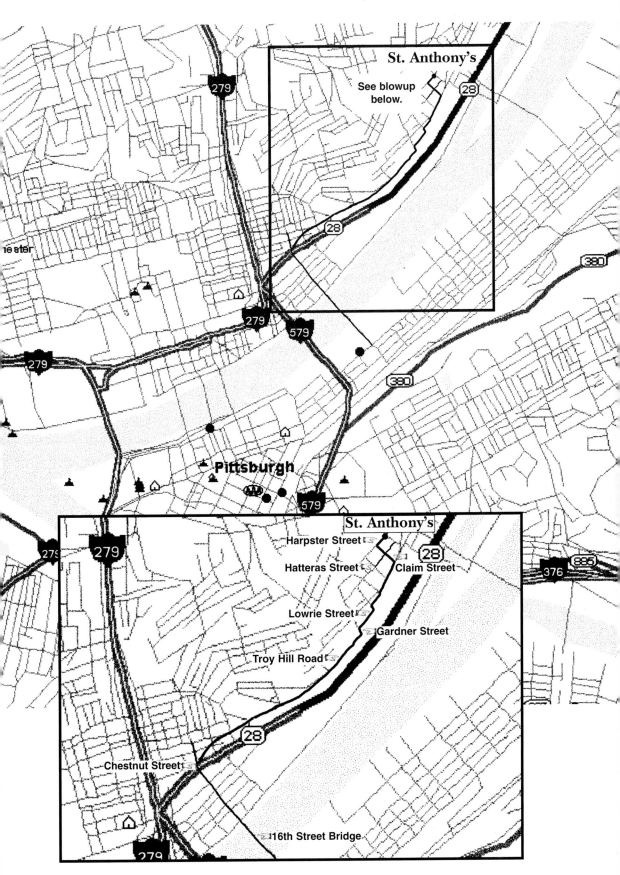

St. Anthony's

See blowup
below.

Pittsburgh

St. Anthony's

Harpster Street

Hatteras Street   Claim Street

Lowrie Street

Gardner Street

Troy Hill Road

Chestnut Street

116th Street Bridge

ST. ANTHONY'S CHAPEL
SCHEDULE

CHAPEL

Tuesday - Thursday - Saturday: 1 p.m. – 4 p.m.

Sunday: 11 a.m. to 4 p.m. with a Tour Guide Present

* NOTE - THE CHAPEL IS CLOSED ON MOST HOLIDAYS

For Guided Tour Scheduling call 323-9504

CHAPEL SHOP AND MUSEUM

Tuesday - Thursday - Saturday - Sunday: 1 p.m. – 4 p.m.

CHAPEL SERVICES

8:30 a.m. – Mass and Novena

7:30 p.m. – Novena and Benedication

STATIONS OF THE CROSS

7:30 p.m. – Fridays of Lent

3:00 p.m. – Sundays in Lent

THE THIRTEEN TUESDAY DEVOTION

Begins 13 Tuesdays before the Feast of St. Anthony, June 13

Special prayers are added to the Novena Prayers for each week of the 13 Tuesdays.

(This Tradition gets its length because of St. Anthony's Feast on the 13th of June.)

TRIDUUM OF ST. ANTHONY

June 11-12-13

Usually Preached by a Franciscan